In the Valley of the Shadow of Death

In the
Valley
of the
Shadow
of Death

Honest conversations
from life's final journey

RANDY BREWER

BIG SNOWY
Media

In the Valley of the Shadow of Death: Honest conversations from life's final journey

. . . .

Library of Congress Cataloging-in-Publication Data
Brewer, Randy Wayne, 1961—
In the Valley of the Shadow of Death: Honest conversations from life's final journey
Big Snowy Media
1. Religion
2. Spirituality

ISBN 978-0-578-82949-4

Printed in the United States of America

10 9 8 7 6 5 4 3 2 1

To my *Good Shepherd* who, even while I walk
in the valley of the shadow of death, I do so without fear.
He has not left me. In fact, He leads me on
and through . . . to the other side.

Contents

Foreword

C.S. Lewis said that Christianity creates, rather than solves, the problem of pain.

His argument is simple: If there is a God, and He is all-powerful and all-loving, then how can He allow the people He loves to suffer?

On the surface, the dilemma is either God is not all-loving, or He is not all-powerful. This is the problem Christians have to solve, a problem that other religions that do not believe in a personal and loving God don't have to face. These religions simply believe that pain is a part of life, that it is neither good nor bad; it just is. And they don't believe in a personal God who cares about your suffering, so there is no one to complain to about your troubles.

Christianity is different.

Christians believe in a God who cares about you so much that He knows the number of hairs on your head. Your life matters to Him, and if you are in pain, that matters, too. If you, like Lewis, have ever wrestled with the problem of pain, then you have come to the right place by picking up this book.

Randy starts the chapter *Inside the Fires of Sorrow* with the statement, "There aren't enough books on the theology of suffering." I couldn't agree more. In order to address the problem of pain, we have to have a theology of suffering. Fortunately, the book you are about to read is one of the best theologies of suffering I have come across in a long time. It's not an academic study of suffering but a first-hand account of someone in the midst of suffering who has a real relationship with a loving God.

In my experience as a clinical psychologist for more than 25 years, I have learned that most of the important problems that people have in life are not solved but managed. The majority of the time we don't get simple solutions to big problems. We are instead forced to develop the courage and faith to live with struggles that we cannot fully understand. On top of that, we rarely get our problems resolved exactly the way we want. I think the Apostle Paul was getting at this when he said, "For we live by faith, not by sight" (2 Cor. 5:7).

Martin Luther developed what he called the "theology of the cross," based on the passage in the Old Testament where Moses asks God if he can see God's face. We all know God's response: "… no one may see me and live" (Ex. 33: 20). Instead, God covered Moses in the cleft of a rock and passed by saying, "I will remove my hand and you will see my back, but my face must not be seen."

Luther constructs his theology of suffering based upon this event. His conclusion is that looking straight into the face of God would be too much glory for any of us to handle in this life. It would literally kill us. Instead, God has made the world such that the most profound experience of God comes not when things are going gloriously well, but when things are not going well at all, or in those moments that Luther calls the back side of God. Luther believed this to be the way of the cross.

When does God become most real to any of us?

When things are going well, when we get our way, or when our problems are somewhere in the distant background of our lives? No, it is more consistently the case that God is felt to be most powerfully present to us when we are most in need of help. Luther thought that God is most real to us when we find Him in the midst of our suffering.

If you can find God there, you will believe in the reality of God anywhere. Just like Jesus on the cross, suffering is not a sign of God's abandonment (even though it felt like it to Jesus and certainly can feel like that to us at times), but it is the pathway to experiencing God in the most real way possible in this life. Luther thought that this truth was so painful to most people that they end up turning away from God at precisely the exact moment when He is most likely to be powerfully present to us—when we are in pain.

Randy explains this powerful truth in his book using the example of his own life to do it. He says, "Scripture doesn't promise believers escape from life's challenges … if you believe that you will be quickly disillusioned." He also reminds us of what C.S. Lewis said: "God whispers to us in our pleasures, speaks to us in our conscience, and shouts in our pain." And he points out that Jesus himself suffered through all the stages of grief just like we do.

A mature life does not have a naïve understanding of suffering in this world, nor of the God who made it. There may be no solution to the problem of pain in this life, but God has given us a powerful way to manage it. Randy points it out in the Psalm 23: "Even though I walk through the valley of the shadow of death, I will fear no evil, for you are with me."

Psychologists have known for years that any trauma, or any suffering, is made more manageable if we do not have to endure it alone. We are relational creatures, and thankfully we have a God who is willing to be there with us in our suffering to make it possible for us to withstand it. Randy has given us a gift. He has offered us a theology of suffering, not just with his ideas about the subject, but by living it out as an example for all of us with his life.

DR. MARK W. BAKER
Pasadena, California

Introduction

In my previous book, *Finding My Voice*, I mentioned how I created an email support list and received some of the most encouraging replies. But as the list grew I decided to take my health updates off email and begin a blog. It was a more efficient way for me to share my latest medical news with people in various countries. The blog morphed from a medical update into a personal expression of what I was learning, my insights in "real time".

That has also formed the basis for this book: months of medical updates and personal biblical insights. The book is a progression of painful, honest and often challenging questions. Some aimed at God and others at myself. Many challenging my beliefs. Ultimately, it is a book of deep self-reflection. Based on some of the later insights, I might prefer to go back and edit the earlier notes...but I will let them be. They were honest struggles at a particular point in time. I have left these unvarnished insights as originally written.

I have often felt a kinship with the apostle Paul. In many ways we were raised similarly, into legalistic religion and leadership in the church. I went to Bible college and seminary. I was a zealot. Though I never persecuted the church or signed off on any death warrants, I can claim with Paul, in his first letter to Timothy, that I am the "chief of sinners" (1 Tim. 1:15). Speaking of Timothy, Paul spent years discipling him into church leadership. I too, have discipled many young people like Timothy.

Paul met Timothy when he was in his teens. When Timothy was about 21 years old, he jumped at the chance to accompany Paul on various church-planting and outreach trips. For years Paul and Timothy, along with Silas, Luke and others, served together as evangelists and church-planters. Paul then left Timothy in Ephesus to tend to a new, young church. Paul's first letter to Timothy was all about the character and gifts that should be exemplified in church leaders, how to deal with nay-sayers and encouraging Timothy not to feel disqualified because he was only 30+ years old.

Several years later, when he was under house arrest in Rome, Paul wrote his second letter to Timothy. This was a much more personal letter. Paul was far less concerned with the "how to's" in the church but instead left Timothy with very clear admonition to stay close to the word of God. In 2 Timothy 2:15, KJV, Paul wrote, "Study to show thyself approved unto God, a workman that needeth not to be ashamed, rightly dividing the word of truth." Paul was saying, if you remember anything I've done or said, God's word is what matters most. Don't just read it. Study it. Understand it. And in 2 Timothy 3:16 he added, "All Scripture is breathed out by God and profitable for teaching, for reproof, for correction, and for training in righteousness." Paul emphasized the capability of the word of God.

And, finally, at the end of this second letter, Paul passes the torch to Timothy. "I have fought the good fight, I have finished the race, I have kept the faith. Henceforth, there is laid up for me the crown of righteousness, which the Lord, the righteous judge, will award to me on that day, and not only to me but also to all who have loved his appearing" (2 Tim. 4:7-8).

Paul knew what Jesus meant when he said "heaven and earth may pass away but my words will never pass away" (Matt. 24:35).

The progression from Paul's first letter to Timothy and his second letter is obvious. And like Paul, I recognize that my life and ministry are coming to a close. I have fought the good fight, I have kept the faith, and I am rounding the last turn in my race. And here's the essence of my manifesto, what I want remembered. The word of God stands forever. I've sought to understand it, live it and share it. I've failed regularly. Thank God for grace. Now it's your turn.

My Current Health and Treatment

May 19, 2019

I believe in a God who heals, using natural means as well as miracles. My Bible says, He is the same yesterday, today and forever. He healed then. He can and does heal today. God is a healer not an afflicter. He does not give people diseases. Nor is sickness caused by a lack of faith or unconfessed sin (see John 9). Indeed, God only asks of us faith the size of a mustard seed, not a faith we muster. Sickness is part of the human condition in a fallen world, a world in which we will have trouble, even as we have been adopted into a new kingdom. Jesus tells us rain falls on the just and unjust alike. The question is not whether I truly believe all this, but

MEDICAL UPDATE * I've been dealing with cancer since my initial diagnosis in March 2012. Surgery, radiation, a barrage of procedures, biopsies and a couple of trial drug treatments have racked my body and compromised my voice, swallowing and breathing.

"But you don't look sick." I hear this all the time, a backhanded compliment. Unfortunately, the cancer has attacked my lungs, and is slowly suffocating me. I am tired and lack energy. I have trouble focusing and my sleep is not restful.

I have accepted my condition as honestly and openly as possible but have not resigned myself to it. Instead, I have poured the entire

what will I do with these beliefs?
I pray. I seek God. I ask Him to take this horrible disease away. I ask Him to guide me. To give me endurance. I know His grace (mercy) is enough for me to walk through the flames. And even if they burn me, I will not concede to fear or bitterness.

Even Jesus, God's only son, prayed for any way other than an early, painful and undeserved death. But, ultimately, he trusted in his Father's plan. Jesus accepted his human condition, his bodily limitations and afflictions, which culminated in his death. And so, like Jesus, I accept my condition. I trust God's plan for me. I must. What good is it to believe only when things are good? That's not faith.

*I believe we live in a fallen world
and even though we, as Christians,
have been adopted into a new kingdom,
yet in this world we WILL have trouble...
as it rains on the just and unjust alike.*

process into my first book, *Finding My Voice*. It recounts the diagnosis, treatment and removal of rare "head and neck" cancer (Adenoid Cystic Carcinoma or ACC) from my trachea, only to have it metastasize to my lungs. ACC is rare, incurable and terminal. But it is growing slowly, giving me time to live fully and trust God, while pursuing all medical options.

These options include modern medicine, which has granted me more than seven years of "missionary travels" around the world. I have also delved into several non-traditional approaches: diets, acupuncture, an herbalist, naturopathic supplements and lifestyle changes.

My passion for life is undiminished even as I feel the pain of this slow-growing disease. I have pains in my chest and lungs and lower back. I can't run, and even a quick climb up the stairs winds me. It's hard to accept for a gym-rat like me.

I've been asking a number of medical professionals, the best in the field, for their recommendations. Their recommendation is to make me nearly dead to keep me alive as long as possible. This is what chemo does. It brings you to the brink of death in an attempt to slow the cancer's growth. The goal is not to cure the cancer but to buy me time. I might get several more months, maybe a year. Medical advancements offer glimmers of hope with targeted drug trials coming on the scene all the time. These trials are not chemo but more genomic-specific meds aimed at genes that have been identified in my tumors. Thankfully, miraculously it seems, I was granted approval for a trial that will start in a few weeks. Please pray!

Meanwhile, I'm no hero of the faith. I've asked why. I agonize over it. I have begged God for a miracle. Here. Now. I have bargained with God. "I need more time. I have more work to do. I'm finally getting into my stride." I'm sad. I'm mad. I'm NOT ok with any of this.

It's not that I'm afraid of death. Not remotely. But I dread dying. Dying is the ugly part of death, for me a slow suffocation. But still I rest. Even in my turmoil. I have a deep inner calm. A peace.

I marvel at this peace that can only come from God. "My peace I give to you." It's a peace of knowing no matter my future on the planet, I have a savior in Jesus, who destroyed

*What good is it to believe only
when things are good?
That's not faith.*

death by his death, and has prepared an everlasting home for me. I remain confident in his promise. Death is not the end, but the beginning of a new mode of life.

Friends, Jesus tells us he is the doorway through death and into abundant life (John 10). If you have not yet accepted Jesus as your Lord and Savior (and I'm not talking about church or religion or some rule-based God you may have learned about in Sunday school), I hope my life and my love for you, despite my many personal failures, will cause you to seek Him. Because if you do…if you truly seek after the only one true God, you WILL find Him. And when you do, you'll know He has been seeking after you from before time. That's our loving God.

Surrender Is Not Retreat!

May 27, 2019

My friends encourage me not to give up, even as the disease progresses. Defeat is not an option, I tell them. Scripture says that the sting of death has been defeated, so no matter what, I can't lose—even if I should die. At the same time, I am learning a lot about surrender. Surrender is not defeat; it's faith in the sovereignty of God, who is on His throne. I live at and for His pleasure. He knows what I don't.

This gives me hope. Hope is an unbreakable chain attached to God, who is my anchor. Hope leads to surrender, which is not natural for us. We are constantly tempted

MEDICAL UPDATE ✱ The clinical trial is set to start June 10th. It's a Phase 1 trial which means little is known about side-effects. This is "gene therapy" administered through pills, 24 big pills a day (12 twice a day). I'll have some pre-tests (CT, EKG and labs) for the next two weeks before I start the trial. If it's working, I could feel better within a couple of weeks. A follow up CT scan in six weeks will confirm effectiveness. I will be monitored closely for any adverse reaction. I trust this trial works—that God uses the meds to do His miracle. I pray for ZERO side-effects and that I am able to swallow all those pills.

At this point I feel pain in my back and chest. Breathing and talking

to think that we are sufficient unto ourselves, that we have life in ourselves. So, we cling to it. Hope gives me reason to let go, and put all my faith in God. Faith is the confidence of what I hope for and the assurance about what I do not yet see.

Life is temporal. It always ends in death, so clinging to it is pointless. My hope is in a life beyond this one, a future with God. My hope is in knowing that my God is a good father who has the best plans for me—now and forever. And my faith is that He will do it. Even while I struggle now, I have confidence God always delivers on His promises.

Don't get me wrong. Death is tragic. It's the last enemy (1 Cor. 15:26). But encompassed by God's sovereignty, death becomes the means by which we return to God, and become

I am learning a lot about surrender. Surrender is not defeat. Surrender says I believe in the total sovereignty of God.

are tough. Even harder is the loss of things I love to do. I can no longer speak publicly. I cannot make phone calls (more than a couple minutes). I can't exercise much.

I take stock daily of what I do have. I'm alive. I remain hopeful. If you follow me on IG, you've seen this in my various activities. By the grace of God, I live the best life possible each day. What you see on social media is my best self, not the struggle. No one's going to "like" a video of me at the hospital surrounded by doctors, or lying down at home swathed in heating packs and ice packs. This is not a pity-party. I just want to be honest.

Even while I struggle now,
God always delivers on His promises.
I have confidence in this...
I have faith.

complete, fully human. God appoints death just as He gives life. Surrendering to death is surrendering to God.

However, this doesn't mean that I won't continually ask God for His miraculous healing so that I can remain here to serve Him and you. Until my "graduation day," I remain hopeful with every breath.

Like the apostle Paul, I can say the following:

> For to me, to live is Christ and to die is gain. If I am to go on living in the body, this will mean fruitful labor for me. Yet what shall I choose? I do not know! I am torn between the two: I desire to depart and be with Christ, which is better by far; but it is more necessary for you that I remain in the body. Convinced of this, I know that I will remain, and I will continue with all of you for your progress and joy in the faith, so that through my being with you again your boasting in Christ Jesus will abound on account of me. (Phil. 1:21-26)

Like Paul I want to remain and continue with all of you. This includes friends around the world. If you know me, you know that hope doesn't always give me serenity. I'm terribly frustrated with my condition. It hurts. I ask God "Why?"

I get mad. I yell. It's one reason I write. Writing about it is honest, raw emotion. As I struggle to understand, I thank God for His grace. Please also extend me mercy as I walk this journey.

The Dichotomy of Failing Health and an Expanding Ministry

June 13, 2019

T he physical challenges are frustrating. Breathing is labored and speaking leaves me in pain. But intense pain also intensifies my sense of purpose wrapped up in God's larger purpose. God is good. He is faithful. I feel like the apostle Paul who spoke about his "thorn in the flesh...a messenger of Satan" (2 Cor. 12). While I pray for God to take my "thorn" away, I am aware it has also caused me to double down on my worldwide ministry with sponsor "kids" in Africa, Indonesia, Japan, China and elsewhere. Suffering has helped inspire two books about the lessons I've learned

MEDICAL UPDATE * I've started the "gene therapy" clinical trial. It's too early to report about any outcomes, but I've had no noticeable side-effects so far. That's good. The doctors are optimistic the drug will stop the cancer growth in my lungs. I'm finding a way to swallow all 24 pills each day, for 21 days, and then a week off, followed by a second

in the midst of my illness. (Shameless plug: Please consider getting your own copies at Amazon and when you do, write a review!)

I recently read the following Bible text below from 2 Corinthians 4:7-12; 16-18:

> But we have this treasure in jars of clay, to show that the surpassing power belongs to God and not to us. We are afflicted in every way, but not crushed; perplexed, but not driven to despair; persecuted, but not forsaken; struck down, but not destroyed; always carrying in the body, the death of Jesus, so that the life of Jesus may also be manifested in our bodies.
>
> For we who live are always being given over to death for Jesus' sake, so that the life of Jesus also may be manifested in our mortal flesh.
>
> So death is at work in us, but life in you.

*While my broken body is failing,
my ministry is expanding.
My outer self is wasting away but
my inner self is being renewed
day by day.*

three-week dosage. A CT scan in about two months will tell us if the pills have worked. After I get through that, I'll focus on restoring the damage done thus far to my voice, swallowing and breathing. Thanks for praying.

*Careers end, relationships fail,
bank accounts dwindle and health
falters. The only hope we have
is the eternal God.*

⁣⁣⁣⁣⁣⁣⁣⁣⁣⁣⁣⁣⁣⁣⁣⁣⁣⁣⁣⁣⁣⁣⁣⁣⁣⁣⁣⁣⁣⁣⁣⁣

So we do not lose heart. Though our outer self is wasting away, our inner self is being renewed day by day. For this light momentary affliction is preparing for us an eternal weight of glory beyond all comparison, as we look not to the things that are seen but to the things that are unseen. For the things that are seen are transient, but the things that are unseen are eternal.

I couldn't agree more. While my broken body keeps failing, my ministry is expanding. My outer self is wasting away, but my inner self is being renewed day by day.

This is the mystery of faith in Christ.

I know some may be thinking; "Your belief is your coping mechanism, Randy, to help you deal with the bleak reality of cancer and death." However, my faith goes much deeper than any cancer diagnosis. It gives me hope when medical reports don't. And frankly, even in perfect health, Jesus is my one true hope. We all need hope. Careers end, relationships fail, bank accounts dwindle and health falters. The only hope we have is the eternal God.

This new song by Lincoln Brewster, "While I Wait," speaks perfectly to my situation.

I am so thankful for each of you. I've gotten calls and

messages and even some out-of-area friends have made special visits. Thank you all. I am deeply grateful. What a joy to know I have prayer warriors, friends and family all over the world. I am not alone in this fight. And trust me, that's a real blessing.

Be blessed. Be well!

Thank God for Cancer?

June 25, 2019

"Rejoice always, pray without ceasing, give thanks in all circumstances; for this is the will of God in Christ Jesus for you" (I Thes. 5:16-18).

I've been taught that we can give thanks in everything but not for everything. Now I wonder if this summary insight misses the point. If the distinction between in and for might be false. What's the difference really, since God pretty much lets it all happen. I've shared with you what I believe about the sovereignty of God. God is completely in control, and He alone is on the throne. I say that I trust Him and His plans for me. But what does it mean to trust in His sovereignty? How can it be more than a spiritual catchphrase and really take more residence in my life?

MEDICAL UPDATE ✳ I've been on this Phase 1 clinical trial for 13 days now. The trial consists of taking 24 pills per day and spending one day a week in the hospital for follow-up tests and observations. The doctor says I need to give the trial at least two months to find out if it's working. I have been enduring the side effects: hives, muscle aches, stomach-ache and a general feeling of "yuck." The medical tests show everything to be fine, but my body can sense what the

If God is sovereign over all, perhaps I need to thank Him for all—health and sickness. Because all of it accomplishes His purpose. I'm wrestling with how to reconcile my reality with God's sovereignty.

If I believe God is in charge and knows what He's doing, then my attitude should follow my belief. I can be grateful for His purpose, accomplished in me and through me. This includes my sickness and pain. I can rejoice in my trials with the recognition that God allows them for the greater good.

Part of me is already there. I do trust God. I know in my head and my heart that He is a good God and has the best plans for my future. I trust what He's doing for me, but I don't like how He's doing it, and what it's doing to me. This is my dilemma and I am not alone. David wrote in Psalms 13...

How long, O Lord? Will you forget me forever?
How long will you hide your face from me?
How long must I take counsel in my soul
and have sorrow in my heart all the day?
How long shall my enemy be exalted over me?
Consider and answer me, O Lord my God;
light up my eyes, lest I sleep the sleep of death,

tests don't show. Something's amiss. When you've driven a car for a long time, you know when something isn't right. It just feels "off" even though the mechanic checks the oil and the belts, kicks the tires and says you're good to go. So, I press on with the prayer and hope that the medicine is targeting the NTRK gene which is thought to be the "driver" of my cancer. Thanks for your prayers and well wishes.

*I know in my head and my heart
that He is a good God and has
the best plans for my future,
but I still don't like cancer and
all that it is doing to me.*

lest my enemy say, "I have prevailed over him,"
lest my foes rejoice because I am shaken.
But I have trusted in your steadfast love;
my heart shall rejoice in your salvation.
I will sing to the Lord,
because He has dealt bountifully with me.

David walked the tightrope of anguish, sorrow, frustration and even the fear of death but still resolved with faith, hope and praise. Likewise, I pray; How long, Lord? How long will I be plagued with this disease? My body is tortured with pain, and my mind is heavy with many thoughts. But you, oh Lord are the keeper of my soul. And you only, my God, can heal, restore and save me. My heart belongs to you. You have done great things and I will thank you for all of it, the good and the bad, because you are the sovereign Lord who makes peace and creates woe (Isa. 45:7).

Jesus Is Always Right on Time!

July 6, 2019

"Be joyful in hope, patient in affliction, faithful in prayer."
Romans 12:12

A colleague and friend from my company recently shared this scripture with me. She unexpectedly lost her husband to a heart attack two weeks ago. Yet even in her grief, she took time to encourage me with these words from Apostle Paul to the Romans.

We don't know what "affliction" Paul was referring to when he penned his letter to the Christians in Rome, but we can speculate. At the time, Christian converts were facing persecution from the Jews as well as the Romans. Jealous of the rise of Christianity and fearing the loss of political

MEDICAL UPDATE *   I completed my first 21-day cycle on the clinical trial meds. I have a week off before starting another cycle of 24 pills a day—for another 21 days.

The meds make me feel like I have the flu, but I can gut it out. There is no indication of how it is working, and the cancer progress-

power, both sought to undermine new believers. Christians were marginalized, harassed, imprisoned and killed.

My suffering pales by comparison to these early Christians. And my impatience is far greater, I'm sure. I want a cure and I want to feel good NOW.

When I have to be at the hospital all day I bark at the nurses and point at the clock. When I am at my worst this scripture reminds me to trust God's timing and not get anxious. His plans are always perfect and never determined by our timeframe.

When Lazarus dies (John 11), his sister, Martha, lashes out at Jesus: if you had been here, my brother would not have died!"

Picture the scene. As the minutes turn to hours, Martha paces, agonizing over her brother and watching down the road for Jesus. She had seen Him do this for others. But not for her, for Martha and Lazarus, Jesus' closest friends.

*At the core, it seems Martha
just didn't trust Jesus.
She couldn't believe He knew more
than she did.*

es. I have significant discomfort in my chest, and my breathing is labored. I will have a throat procedure next week to deal with inflammation in my airway, which will hopefully help with breathing.

These challenges have become routine, but I will keep my head up and my eyes on Jesus. Thanks for your concern and support.

That's Jesus. Always on time.
His plans can be trusted.
So I will be patient as I wait on Him
with my challenges.

IIIIIIIIIIIIIIIIIIIIIIIIIIIIIIIIIIIIIIIIIIIIIIIIIIIIIII

Why isn't he here?

Martha was struggling to trust Jesus, while holding out hope that "even now you can ask God to do something." When Jesus responds that Lazarus will rise again, in exasperation Martha says, "Sure, at the last day."

We can imagine her thinking, "I want him alive NOW, but it's too late for that." Martha trusted Jesus but not completely. There was an implicit demand for what she wanted. She knew better than Jesus. She didn't trust his timing until Jesus thundered right on time: "Lazarus come out."

That's Jesus. Always on time. His plans can be trusted. So, I will be patient as I wait on Him with my challenges. When I get anxious (and I will!) or impatient, may I rest in the confidence of knowing He is securely on the throne. He is always right on time.

The Heart
of the Matter

July 15, 2019

E agles singer, Don Henley, had a solo hit called "Heart of the Matter." [©] The chorus lyrics read...

I've been trying to get down
to the heart of the matter.
But my will gets weak,
and my thoughts seem to scatter.
But I think it's about forgiveness,
Forgiveness.
Even if, even if you don't love me anymore.[1]

Henley sings about choosing forgiveness in response

MEDICAL UPDATE *

On July 11th I began my second 21-day cycle of the trial medication. I'm swallowing the daily dose of 24 pills more easily. The medicine still leaves me feeling like I have a low-grade flu, thankfully the only side effect. My medical team tests and observes me every-other week. On July 10th I had a successful throat procedure to

to a broken relationship. A good decision. Likewise, Jesus encouraged us to choose to forgive. In the famous Lord's Prayer, He said, "And forgive us our debts, as we also have forgiven our debtors."

In Matthew 6:14-15, Jesus reinforces our role in forgiveness and the consequence of not forgiving: "For if you forgive men their trespasses, your heavenly Father will also forgive you. But if you do not forgive men their trespasses, neither will your Father forgive your trespasses."

As I've pondered this, I realize I need forgiveness. Inadvertently, and sometimes on purpose, I've hurt others. I also need to forgive. Everyone's made mistakes, but we only have to take responsibility for our own mistakes.

I grew up around alcoholism and addiction. As a result, I'm familiar with the 12-steps. Step 8 deals with forgiveness: Make a list of all persons we have harmed and become willing to make amends to them all. To forget what lies behind (as the apostle Paul puts it), you must sometimes bring it to

> *Make a list of all persons we have harmed and become willing to make amends to them all.*

reduce swelling in my airway and allow me to breathe better. I still experience shortness of breath and pain when I try to breathe deeply. A CT scan on August 7th will determine if the medicine is stopping the cancer's growth. Pray. Believe.

*Forgiveness releases both parties.
You and me. That's why Jesus
tied giving and receiving forgiveness
together. You can't have one
without the other.*

||||||||||||||||||||||||||||||||||||||||||||||||||||||||||

memory and deal with it.

I like making lists, so I figured, no problem. But this list wouldn't stop.

It was a painful retrospective, not only of my mistakes but of my shortcomings. For example, I was not a great son, brother, uncle, nephew or cousin to my family. I could make excuses. I won't. Please forgive me. As a young, naive church leader, I tried to be an effective minister, but my unresolved hurts caused me to fail. I have not always been a true friend. I sincerely thought I was. However, in putting my needs before others I hurt my friends. I am truly sorry. I never intended to hurt you. After a lot of hard work, I am now living the best, most honest life I can, while still being a flawed human.

And I must also forgive. As I've enjoyed the complete grace and mercy of God and forgiveness for my sins, so too I need to extend the grace of forgiveness to others. To those whose actions against me left me bruised and scarred, I release you from my grip of unforgiveness and bitterness. I will not hold these matters any longer. I forgive you.

Jesus instructed his disciples to forgive seventy times

seven. In other words, constantly. The work of love is forgiveness. This is how God loves us, by constantly forgiving
our continual transgressions. As Charles Spurgeon said,
"God is more ready to forgive me than I am ready to offend."

Make a list of all persons we have harmed and become
willing to make amends to them all.

Forgiveness releases both parties. You and me. That's why
Jesus tied giving and receiving forgiveness together. You
can't have one without the other.

Let the Pages Turn

August 8, 2019

I praise you, for I am fearfully and wonderfully made.
Wonderful are your works;
my soul knows it very well.
My frame was not hidden from you,
when I was being made in secret,
intricately woven in the depths of the earth.
Your eyes saw my unformed substance;
in your book were written, every one of them,
the days that were formed for me,
when as yet there was none of them. (Ps. 139:14-16)

This scripture gives me great peace. God not only made

MEDICAL UPDATE *   I had my CT scan on Wednesday and met with the doctor to-day. Unfortunately, the clinical trial has not been successful. The cancer is continuing to grow. I have a few treatment options to consider and will discuss those with family and medical staff before moving forward.

To look at me, you might not think I'm sick. But spend any amount of time with me and you'll see me gasping for breath and tiring just walking a short distance. I struggle and wheeze when I talk. I'm not

me, He wrote me into His book, every day of my life, before I was even formed. This means God has incorporated the book of my life into His book. Yours too. Every day, hour and minute. Each high and low. The beginning and the end of our life is penned by God. So, while I am challenged by my declining physical condition and frustrated to be completely powerless over my disease, I know the author has written even that into His book.

I imagine my book to be like a courtroom drama. I'm on the stand being grilled by an accusing prosecutor.

While I am challenged by my declining physical condition and frustrated to be completely powerless over my disease, I rest knowing that God is not at all surprised by any of it. He has written every day in His book on my life.

seeking pity. Just stating reality. Things are not getting better. This aggressive cancer is progressing as expected.

Some ask me how they should pray. Pray for endurance to manage the pain and physical challenges. Pray that I have wisdom in deciding my future treatment options. Pray that I always reflect God's love. Pray that I end well, whenever that time comes. Remember, to be absent from the body is to be present with the Lord (2 Cor. 5:8).

These experiences and the wonderful people I am meeting along the way were written in my life's book by God Himself. I could never have written something this fascinating for myself.

⁣||||||||||||||||||||||||||||||||||||||||||||||||||||||||

Oh, I'm guilty. No question. And I deserve judgment. But before I can utter a word, my defense attorney says he's taken all my guilt upon himself and has already suffered the death sentence on my behalf.

With these words, the judge bangs his gavel and exclaims, "Not guilty! Case dismissed." The prosecutor is left with no case. No charges remain. I am a free man.

Talk about a Hollywood ending.

The truth is, my story has been more interesting than any Hollywood movie, with more twists and turns than a screenwriter could imagine. These past few chapters have been far richer and more rewarding than anything I could have dreamed.

Just three days ago I visited a grade school in Tangerang, Indonesia, where around 200 children from the impoverished neighboring community attend school through the support of World Harvest donors.

I got to meet Clara, an 8th grader who my colleagues at Brewer Direct sponsored in my name as my Christmas gift. Through a translator, I learned that she has two younger brothers and enjoys English and wants to be a doctor.

There's Kristo, a 12-year-old boy I have been sponsoring

since 2014, who ran into the room and gave me a hug. We talked (with a translator) about his grades, school, favorite sports. Kristo's mom and younger brother were with him and said they were praying for my health. The kids enjoyed a special concert by Anointed Crushers from Uganda, Africa followed by a special lunch. What a rewarding day.

How can I compare my "momentary affliction" to this?

These experiences and the wonderful people I am meeting along the way were written in my life's book by God Himself. I could never have written something this fascinating for myself. Only He could do this. And so it is with my health and disease. God remains the author of it all. My response is to trust Him and let the pages turn.

You know I love music. Here's a song that touches me by the band Carrollton.

I Will Trust [©]
Though the arrows fly
Though the terrors rage
Though there be no answers for the prayers I've prayed

I will trust
I will trust
I will trust in You
When I face the pain
That is sure to come
When deep sorrow rolls like waves I can't outrun
I will trust
I will trust

I will trust in You

You're my refuge
And my defense
How You love me I will trust

You're my fortress
And You're my strength
Oh, how You love me I will trust

You're my refuge
And my defense
How You love me I will trust

You're my fortress
And You're my strength
Oh, how You love me I will trust

I will trust
I will trust
I will trust in You
I will trust
I will trust
I will trust in You[2]

Will You Perish or Just Fall Asleep?

August 28, 2019

The apostle Paul said, if Christ was not raised from the dead, there is no hope for Christians when they die, because there would be no resurrection for them either. Christians would be "most pitied" for believing an illusion. The gospel Paul had preached to them must not have been true. (This is my paraphrase from 1 Corinthians 15: 1-19).

MEDICAL UPDATE ∗   I've seen a lot of doctors since ending my latest clinical trial and have been trying to navigate my "next steps." Adenoid Cystic Carcinoma (ACC) is especially challenging. Doctors know little about it, and there are no known cures. Metastatic ACC in the lungs is even harder to treat, but there's always hope.

I fight this battle on two fronts. The first is my throat, where no cancer remains, but where past surgeries and radiation treatment have left my breathing and speech seriously compromised. I've had multiple procedures, but nothing has helped for very long.

I've started using a C-PAP machine at night, but I still wheeze and cough all day long. Difficult breathing is affecting my sleep, sapping my energy and restricting my daily activities. So, I am making an appointment with my throat surgeon (from seven years ago) who knows my throat anatomy better than anyone. Please pray that he has supernatural wisdom to help me.

I love Paul. He doesn't mince words. People at the church in Corinth were beginning to wonder about the reality of resurrection. Some of their family and friends were dying, and hadn't been resurrected. Perhaps this story of Jesus being raised wasn't true. The Corinthians' faith in an afterlife began to wane. Paul didn't try to convince them of the resurrection. He simply pointed out the utter hopelessness of life without it. A life as bleak as death. They are to be pitied because their dead are lost forever and they remain trapped in their sins.

Wow! Paul calling it like it is.

If this Jesus stuff is all phony-baloney then yes, I'd be quite scared of death and I'd have a lot of regrets in this life.

|||||||||||||||||||||||||||||||||||||||||||||||||||||

The second battlefield is, of course, my lungs. The growing lesions are deadly and are slowly strangling me. Climbing a flight of stairs leaves me breathless. I met with a pulmonary lung cancer doctor today who suggested we attack the larger lesions with something called radiofrequency ablation (RFA). This may be a way to ease my pain while slowing the spread of cancer in my lungs. This will buy me time. I am waiting to consult with the specialist who performs this procedure.

I just acquired a small oxygen machine to help increase my O2 levels. Managing my health is a full-time job. On top of the chronic pain, I am completely spent. I don't like to complain, but I long for moments of less pain, filled with laughter and the ability to enjoy the simplest pleasures, like relaxing at the beach. And yet, I still travel, squeezing in flights abroad between medical appointments. On these trips I feel the most alive and at peace .

Until the day I "fall asleep"
I will "live for Christ" as best I can.

||||||||||||||||||||||||||||||||||||||||||||||||||

Since I've come face to face with my mortality a few of my friends have asked me if I'm scared. "Do you have any regrets?" they ask. In those moments I reflect on this message from Paul. If this Jesus stuff is all phony-baloney then yes, I'd be scared of death and have a lot of regrets.

But Paul goes on to say in verse 20, "But in fact Christ has been raised from the dead, the first fruits of those who have fallen asleep." Paul states it as fact: Christ has been raised from the dead, and, therefore, those who have died will also be raised and share in heaven.

Christian thinking starts with the reality of the resurrection. The phrase "first fruits" is drawn from the harvest. Christ's resurrection is not a one-off. No, Christ's resurrection is the first basket out of a fertile field, the first taste of the great resurrection harvest to come.

I love how Paul contrasts death without resurrection and death followed by resurrection. It's the difference between perishing and simply falling asleep. Without resurrection, death means we perish, and our lives have been wasted. With it, death is simply falling asleep until that moment we are awakened by our glorious savior Jesus.

So, to my friends I say, I have no fear of falling asleep and no regrets.

This week I had a Brewer Direct board meeting. The board is made of godly business and ministry leaders who come together quarterly to offer their wisdom in leading this organization. Best-selling author Laurie Beth Jones, who serves on my board commented twice about my spirit and positive countenance in spite of these trying times that I face.

"How do you do it?" she asks.

I respond with Philippians 1:21: "To live is Christ and to die is gain." I've said it before. I'm no hero. I continue to agonize over my condition. But I choose to smile and keep my spirits up—and I will myself to bless the Lord, in my weakness. Not always. But this is my desire and my aim. Until the day I "fall asleep" I will "live for Christ" as best I can.

I pray that you know, along with me, that you won't perish when you die. You will only fall asleep with the glorious promise of a resurrection with the return of Jesus.

Planting More Good Fruit

September 24, 2019

I recently hosted a gathering of 19 friends (excluding children), mostly couples ranging in age from mid-20s to mid-50s. The racial mix was colorful, with half a dozen different cultures represented. Many of them met one another for the first time, having only me in common.

After everyone left, I was reminded of the words of Jesus from Matthew 7:15-20:

> Beware of false prophets, who come to you in sheep's clothing but inwardly are ravenous wolves. You will

---

MEDICAL UPDATE
*

As I have shared before, I have two related but distinctly different physical challenges. My throat and my lungs.

In 2012, the cancer was removed from my throat through a radical surgery followed by 33 rounds of radiation. The damage caused by this necessary treatment continues to restrict my speaking and breathing.

The breathing issues have now become severe. This week I consulted my original throat surgeon along with his colleague. Based on their counsel I will have surgery first thing Wednesday morning, October 2nd. If all goes well I'll be back home later the same day. Please pray for the hands of my two surgeons Dr. O'Dell and Dr.

recognize them by their fruits. Are grapes gathered from thornbushes, or figs from thistles? So, every healthy tree bears good fruit, but the diseased tree bears bad fruit. A healthy tree cannot bear bad fruit, nor can a diseased tree bear good fruit. Every tree that does not bear good fruit is cut down and thrown into the fire. Thus you will recognize them by their fruits.

I've had the pleasure of "living life" with these friends, some for a short time and others for many, many years. I've made plenty of mistakes over the years. I've had to apologize a lot. Yet these friends continue to value me. What a blessing. When I doubt myself or feel unworthy, these friends (and others) that I've poured myself into represent the good fruit that I've cultivated throughout my life.

As I continue to move away from my CEO role at Brewer Direct and move into the ambassador role of my foundation, I look forward to investing more time and energy with people and ministries around the world.

Since the inception of the Randy W. Brewer Foundation

Kokot. Pray this procedure is completely successful. Pray that my breathing and voice return to normal.

In 2016, the same cancer was identified in my lungs. I've attempted to stop or slow the growth with three unsuccessful clinical trials. The cancer continues to grow slowly. I have discussed a complete lung transplant, radiation and radiofrequency ablation (RFA). Unfortunately, all of these have been ruled out, leaving only a form of chemotherapy to possibly give me more time by reducing or slowing the cancer's growth. This is still under discussion.

When I doubt myself or feel unworthy, these friends (and others) that I've poured myself into represent the good fruit that I've cultivated throughout my life.

IIIIIIIIIIIIIIIIIIIIIIIIIIIIIIIIIIIIIIIIIIIIIIIIIIIII

in 2018, we've granted hundreds of thousands of dollars to schools, churches, child sponsorship, small businesses in developing nations, more than two dozen university students in Africa, orphan missions in Sri Lanka and Cambodia, capacity building for a non-profit in Compton, CA and even campus ministry in nearby Glendora. Expanding this ministry is truly my life's calling. Planting good seed that bears thirty-, sixty- and a hundred-fold. Even though I'm sick, I continue to live at full capacity.

Let me close with the lyrics of one of my favorite worship songs these days.

Yes, I Will©

I count on one thing
The same God that never fails
Will not fail me now
You won't fail me now
In the waiting
The same God who's never late
Is working all things out
You're working all things out

Yes I will, lift You high in the lowest valley
Yes I will, bless Your name
Oh, yes I will, sing for joy when my heart is heavy
All my days, oh yes I will

And I choose to praise
To glorify, glorify
The Name of all names
That nothing can stand against
And I choose to praise
To glorify, glorify
The Name of all names
That nothing can stand against
And I choose to praise
To glorify, glorify
The Name of all names
That nothing can stand against
And I choose to praise
To glorify, to glorify
The Name of all names
That nothing can stand against [3]

Sufficient for the Day Is Its Own Trouble

October 9, 2019

W hat did Jesus mean when he said, "Therefore do not be anxious about tomorrow, for tomorrow will be anxious for itself. Sufficient for the day is its own trouble" (Matthew 6:34).

This passage was part of a larger teaching generally referred to as The Sermon on the Mount from Matthew 5-7. Having just returned victorious from being tempted in the desert, Jesus formally began his ministry by preaching repentance and choosing his disciples. As he was healing the sick and casting out demons, a large multitude of people

MEDICAL UPDATE ✱ On Wednesday, October 2nd, I underwent throat surgery. This was primarily to open up my airway which had become largely blocked by swelling, paralyzed vocal cords and dried mucus. It's hard to describe the progressive choking sensation, but it truly felt as if my life was being snuffed out.

The procedure was a success!

I was riding my bike the next day. It was an enormous relief to find

started following him. So, he pulled away his disciples and began to teach them.

It's apparent that many others listened as well. Jesus' audience was largely poor, uneducated, sick and ostracized by society. They were oppressed by Roman law and burdened by strict Jewish religious traditions. They couldn't measure up.

Jesus led into the "Don't worry" passage, starting in 6:25, by expounding on the birds of the air and the grass of the field. They don't worry and yet God takes care of them. Therefore, why worry yourselves?

Jesus then adds a caveat. "Sufficient for the day is its own trouble". Jesus did not say to his disciples and the larger group of potential followers, "Follow me and all will be well...no problems." Instead, he admits, as he does later in John 16:33, "Guys, your lives will be challenging. You're going to face difficulties."

Scripture doesn't promise believers escape from life's challenges: suffering, persecution, financial struggles, sickness, disease and the like. If you believe that, you will be quickly disillusioned. Jesus does, however, promise to be a source of strength for us in the midst of trouble. That's how we can "be of good cheer."

out my throat swelling was not related to the cancer in my lungs, as some of my doctors suspected. I can breathe freely again. Other than a wicked sore throat and inability to speak I feel good and ready for the gym. I can't wait to tell my lung doctor about the successful throat surgery. The pressure is off, for now. I will have another CT Scan in mid-November, and we'll discuss next steps after that.

Scripture doesn't promise that believers will escape life's challenges: suffering, persecution, financial struggles, sickness, disease and the like. If you believe that, then you are going to crash and burn when you are hit with something difficult.

llllllllllllllllllllllllllllllllllllllllllllllllllllllll

Given my tremendous physical "troubles", I've asked myself, how do I prevent today's challenges from adversely impacting my life tomorrow? I pray and do my best to "let go and let God" but I still need to press through this challenging path every single day.

Consider the car windshield. Hopefully, it's large and clean, providing a good view of the road ahead. As it deflects the wind, the windshield picks ups nicks, chips, cracks, a Kamikaze bug or two, and bird poop (which always always seems to find your windshield just after a car wash. I'm convinced birds congregate at car wash exits!).

These windshield blemishes can distract our focus, and cause us to lose sight of the road. We can't clearly focus on both the up-close and the distant at the same time.

Perhaps that's what is meant by not worrying about tomorrow. We don't worry about what's going to hit the windshield tomorrow. Instead, we stop and clean off the windshield today. And continue driving, focusing on the road ahead without worrying about upcoming window mishaps.

No matter what challenges you face, big or small, Jesus says, don't overthink them. In the grand scheme of things, they are like little spots on the big windshield. Deal with what's in front of you, but don't worry about what you don't see. There'll be more spots and bug stains. That's life on the road.

Which brings me back to my breathing issues. With no clear explanation or diagnosis, I had worried myself into thinking I had only days or weeks to live. As Jesus said, worrying can't change the outcome of anything. Instead, we can give our worries to God our creator and truly trust in His plan. Easy to say. Hard to do. Sufficient for the day is its own trouble. Live in the moment.

P.S. Please pray for me as I travel to Kenya and Uganda, Africa this Sunday, October 13 through October 28. I have a full schedule and need strength and must remain healthy.

Boasting in Weakness

November 4, 2019

But whatever anyone else dares to boast of—I am speaking as a fool—I also dare to boast of that. Are they Hebrews? So am I. Are they Israelites? So am I. Are they offspring of Abraham? So am I. Are they servants of Christ? I am a better one—I am talking like a madman—with far greater labors, far more imprisonments, with countless beatings, and often near death. Five times I received at the hands of the Jews the forty lashes less one. Three times I was beaten with rods. Once I was stoned. Three times I was

MEDICAL UPDATE It's been over a month since my throat procedure, and my breathing remains pretty good. After my original surgery and radiation in 2012, it's never been great. There's no danger from cancer or other issues in my throat. It's simply frustrating and challenging. Swallowing and speaking are still compromised, and short of God's miraculous touch, that isn't changing.

The lungs, however, are the concern. The cancer tumors continue to grow with no new treatments or trials available for me (at the present). I am currently not on any treatments or meds at all. The doctors want me to have chemotherapy, believing it could help a little (but of course, not cure); but many, including medical practitioners, are

shipwrecked; a night and a day I was adrift at sea; on frequent journeys, in danger from rivers, danger from robbers, danger from my own people, danger from Gentiles, danger in the city, danger in the wilderness, danger at sea, danger from false brothers; in toil and hardship, through many a sleepless night, in hunger and thirst, often without food in cold and exposure. And, apart from other things, there is the daily pressure on me of my anxiety for all the churches. Who is weak, and I am not weak? Who is made to fall, and I am not indignant? (2 Cor. 11:21-29, ESV).

I am being challenged by the Apostle Paul to change my approach, to view my "messenger from Satan" as God's way to keep me humble... so in boasting in my weakness, God gets all the glory for it is only His power that sustains me.

||||||||||||||||||||||||||||||||||||||||||||||||||

encouraging me to avoid chemo. It's the only remaining "Hail Mary" solution the doctors have for me, and with it come a series of further complications. So, I am leaning against chemo.

I'll have a CT Scan on January 7th, 2020 (please mark this date on your prayer calendar), after which I will have further discussions with my medical team. Continue to pray for my endurance. My trip to Uganda and Kenya (and Qatar) was a blessing and God sustained me. People ask what the doctors think of all my traveling? I give them the same answer I give my doctors. I feel better when I travel. I believe God empowers me...so I will keep going as long as He allows me.

*Even while I have faith in His promises
and wait with eager Hope, I WILL
boast in my weakness. It is entirely
His grace and strength that is my
sufficiency. Nothing else.*

||||||||||||||||||||||||||||||||||||||||||||||||||

If anyone else thinks he has reason for confidence in the flesh, I have more: circumcised on the eighth day, of the people of Israel, of the tribe of Benjamin, a Hebrew of Hebrews; as to the law, a Pharisee; as to zeal, a persecutor of the church; as to righteousness under the law, blameless. But whatever gain I had, I counted as loss for the sake of Christ. (Phil. 3:5-7, ESV)

Paul boasted in his heritage. His education. His zeal. And even the persecution and suffering he endured after coming to Christ. Paul is quick to admit he's crazy to brag, because anything he could claim for himself was worthless, counted as loss compared to Christ.

So, why did he boast?

I believe the answer is in 2 Corinthians 11:30; "If I must boast, I will boast of the things that show my weakness." In the next chapter, Paul describes his weakness.

So, to keep me from becoming conceited because of the surpassing greatness of the revelations, a thorn was given me in the flesh, a messenger of Satan to harass me, to keep me from becoming conceited. Three times I pleaded with the Lord about this, that it should leave me. But he said to me, "My grace is sufficient for you, for my power is made perfect in weakness." Therefore, I will boast all the more gladly of my weaknesses, so that the power of Christ may rest upon me. For the sake of Christ, then, I am content with weaknesses, insults, hardships, persecutions, and calamities. For when I am weak, then I am strong. (2 Cor. 12:7-10, ESV)

All Paul's accomplishments, experiences and zeal for God, before and after meeting Jesus, could not alleviate the pain and suffering associated with the "thorn in the flesh". Powerless to change his situation, Paul could only boast in God's grace and goodness and power. Paul was certainly not proud of his affliction; he begged God to remove it. Rather, Paul boasted in God's exhibited power in spite of his own weakness.

This is how Paul remained humble. He was born into the right family, highly educated and capable of doing miraculous exploits for God. Yet, he carried in his body this obvious display of a weakness totally beyond his control.

I see parallels to my situation, although the Apostle Paul has a lot on me. I was born into a Christian family. I went to Bible school and seminary. I can tell of amazing things I've seen and done for God. Like Paul, I tend to rely on my own strength. Like Paul, I remain "harassed" by my disease, and am totally powerless to change my situation. It has weakened me tremendously and at times totally humiliated me.

But I am being challenged by the Apostle Paul to change

my approach, to view my "messenger from Satan" as God's way to keep me humble. So in boasting in my weakness, God gets all the glory. For it is only His power that sustains me.

It is Jesus who allows me to wake up from one day to the next. My pain, my constant coughing and choking, are a constant reminder of my total weakness. It is in Him alone that I have breath. And it is for Him alone that I live.

This is a difficult lesson for me. I continue to ask God to remove this thorn in my flesh (Paul stopped after just three requests). And I beg God for some relief. But even as I place my faith in His promises and wait with eager hope, I WILL boast in my weakness. God's grace and strength are my sufficiency. Nothing else. Doctors have run out of answers. My disease makes no sense. I have blamed myself for too long.

At this time, all I can do is have faith, trusting and hoping in the sovereignty and sufficiency of God. He is on the throne. Not me. Not anyone else. So, join me in boasting in weakness—for in doing so we are made strong.

Suffering Is God's Loud Voice... Telling Me to Go!

November 20, 2019

In the *Problem of Pain*, apologist C.S. Lewis writes, "God whispers to us in our pleasures, speaks in our conscience, but shouts in our pain." And in, *Walking with God through Pain and Suffering*, pastor and author Tim Keller writes, "Believers understand many doctrinal truths in the mind, but those truths seldom make the journey down into the heart except through disappointment, failure and loss.... you don't really know Jesus is all you need until Jesus is all you have."

These two quotes, along with my own recent study of the book of Job, have been challenging me. Recently, my suffering has felt unbearable. The physical pain is not something

MEDICAL UPDATE ✱ I don't have much new to report. I'll have my first follow-up with my throat doctor on December 6 as well as an appointment with my oncologist at USC. I sense my breathing is degrading. I will discuss this with the doctor. My options are another steroid injection

I can easily explain. One morning a week ago as I was making breakfast, I coughed and choked so much I could barely catch my breath. I grabbed my chest, fell to the floor and cried out to God through tears begging for relief. I'm not being overly dramatic, nor am I seeking sympathy. But I'm left to ask: *What is God trying to teach me through all of this? And, am I listening?*

We are all familiar with Job 13:15, "Though he slay me, I will hope in him." But Job also said, "Why did you bring me out of the womb? Would that I had died before any eye had seen me and were as though I had not been, carried from the womb to the grave" (Job 10:18-19).

Job was brutally honest and complained openly to God about his condition. He didn't understand why so much suffering had befallen him. Of course, we like to celebrate the end of the story, after Job recognized God's ultimate sovereignty. Job's health was restored. He had more kids—beautiful children. His fortunes were returned twice over. He lived another 140 years as a blessed man.

Praise the Lord, right?

But wait. His original ten kids were still dead. And for what reason? Why were they killed? What had they done? While I am not trying to exegete all of Job here today, I do resonate with Job's complaints and questions: *Why God?*

in the larynx or a more aggressive procedure in January. I continue to cough, which makes my throat sore. I have a chest CT scan on January 7, which will show how much the cancer has spread in my lungs. Please continue to pray.

When my days are through,
whenever that is, I will also go.
And I'll be gone. Gone from this earth
to spend eternity with God.

llllllllllllllllllllllllllllllllllllllllllllllllll

Why cancer? Why the voice? Why untreatable in the lungs?
Why so much pain? Between the questions, I beg God for relief. I feel stripped and beaten anew each day.

On the heels of all of this I began a week of travel, five flights, four airports, three cities over four days. Some asked me if it was wise to travel while I felt so bad. Interestingly, as I boarded the first flight I began to feel better. Not miraculously. My breathing was still problematic and I still had a cough. But, my head didn't hurt. My back wasn't sore. My chest didn't ache. My ears weren't ringing. Two flights later, landing after midnight in 9-degree weather, I still felt good.

A couple of days later, I took a long flight back to LAX, got stuck in traffic, yet felt fine. The following day I was back to the airport and on yet another plane. And so on. But, I was feeling good. No major pains. As soon as I got home, after flight number five, I started feeling bad again. Is it psychosomatic? I don't think so. Is it stress being at home? Maybe. I do have a lot of responsibilities.

But then I heard God speaking. Not audibly, but in that still small voice: "Go!"

In the past five months I've been in Indonesia, Japan, Uganda, Kenya, Qatar and even Chicago and Indianapolis, and in every instance, when I was away, I felt better. Clearly, before I am gone, I need to keep going!

The gospel of Luke recounts Jesus sending out 72 followers to reach the lost. Luke 10:3 begins with Jesus' command, "Go!" Jesus then promises his disciples that "nothing shall hurt you." This promise is contingent on their going, not their staying. Nothing shall hurt you as you go. As I read this it hits me. "Go Randy!" I feel like Homer Simpson as he hits himself in the head and says "D'oh!" The only way I am going to experience God's peace and wellness is if I go.

This month I am wrapping up my role as CEO of Brewer Direct. This chapter in my life is coming to a close. I am going. In 2020, I will return to Africa, Asia and wherever God sends me to promote His kingdom. I will go. And when my days are through, whenever that is, I will also go. And I'll be gone. Gone from this earth to spend eternity with God.

David Cassidy, iconic 70's pop musician and TV star, died of liver failure at age 67. "So much wasted time," he said just before he died. I don't want to waste any more time. If you've read my book *Releasing Generosity*, you know my goal is to die OBE: Old. Broke. Exhausted. I can only experience OBE as I go. No time to rest. As my trainer and friend Kurt regularly says, "You can rest when you're dead."

Yes, Lord! I am listening. I will go.

Thank you for praying and supporting me through this journey. As I finish this blog post, I am excited about the next chapter...wherever God leads. I'm going.

Staying in the Right Lane

December 11, 2019

Have you ever been driving, starting a lane change when suddenly, seemingly out of nowhere, a car is in your path, causing you quickly to swerve back into your lane? It's called a blind spot. Most cars have blind spots which obstruct a driver's view. We use mirrors to give us a side view into areas out of our sight-lines. Newer cars employ sensors to warn the driver of objects out of immediate view.

Each of us has blind spots in our lives, areas out of view, perspectives hard to see. Our blind spots could be related to any number of areas, including family matters, job choices or school situations. The best way to gain a view into our blind

MEDICAL UPDATE *

I'm writing from Japan, where I'll be until I travel to Thailand for the holidays. As I noted, I'm better when I'm "on the go." Last Friday I saw my throat doctor at Keck/USC Hospital. She and I agreed to reevaluate in January and decide if a more aggressive procedure will help my breathing which has regressed.

I then met with my cancer doctor at USC Norris Cancer Hospital. We discussed an updated list of new clinical trials targeting my version of lung cancer. He agreed with my second cancer doctor from

spots is to have people help us see what we can't see. This takes a great deal of trust. And it takes time, the Bible says.

Proverbs 11:14 says, "Where there is no guidance, a people falls, but in an abundance of counselors there is safety."

In business, a board of directors provides wisdom to the business managers to keep everyone on task. In church ministry we seek a plurality of leadership and elders to bring accountability to the senior pastor. In a democratic governance like America, we have three equal branches of government—the legislative, executive and judicial. This provides "checks and balances" to help prevent a dictatorship. The book of Ecclesiastes 4:12 says "And though a man might prevail against one who is alone, two will withstand him—a threefold cord is not quickly broken."

When our counselors point out a blind spot, it's hard

We all have blind spots and the best way to gain a view into our blind spots is to have people around us to help us see what we can't see.

City of Hope Cancer Hospital that a new clinical trial targeted at my lungs looks like a good possible option for me. The clinical trial is being conducted in Boston, so I expect to fly out in January for a consultation. I also have a CT scan scheduled in early January. So please be praying.

In January I will also try to sell my Monrovia home of 30+ years and settle into my home in Seal Beach.

Jesus chose more than one disciple for a reason. We need others. We need opposing views. We need to be challenged and stretched in our thinking.

||||||||||||||||||||||||||||||||||||||||||||||||||

to look. To acknowledge our blind spots. It's why some churches split and pastors leave to start their own one-off fellowship. (I'd be wary of attending such a church.) And countries run by dictatorships are often difficult to live in because the dictator/leader seeks to ingratiate himself to family and friends instead of truly leading the country.

As I've traveled to a number of Third World and developing nations, I've seen a lot of misguided countries that have tremendous resources, but far too many poor and needy people. Leadership is often myopic (simply stated). And I've also experienced a number of church ministries, operating alone without the covering of wise counsel.

I have taken the Scriptures and these experiences to heart. That's why with my own foundation, I have a board to help guide our funding. It's why almost all our grants are given to established ministries that have their own fiduciary controls.

As I continue to wrestle with health matters and hard choices, I lean on the wisdom of others. These include my brother, Terry, many medical professionals, friends and pastors. It's hard to admit that my emotions cloud my view, creating blind spots. I drift over and I need someone to nudge me into the right lane.

Who in your life is helping you with your blind spots? When they point them out, do you listen? Jesus chose more than one disciple for a reason. We need others. We need opposing views. We need to be challenged and stretched in our thinking. And we need trusted counselors who will speak truth to our blind spots and help us see what may be out of our view.

Let them guide us into the right lane.

My Lawn May Have Weeds... But It Is Well with My Soul

January 11, 2020

My lungs are like a well-manicured lawn with weeds sprouting up in the grass. Unfortunately, there are too many weeds to pull out one-by-one. I watched and wait-

MEDICAL UPDATE ✳ I had a nice time in Japan and Thailand over the holidays. It was great to connect with friends, eat amazing food and actually have some energy for the gym several times. However, even with this reprieve, my throat keeps getting worse, so I am having another surgery (fairly minor) this Wednesday, January 15. Please pray it goes well and gives me the relief I need. I continue to cough, choke and feel like I'm being strangled most of the time, all the result of previous throat cancer treatment. Thankfully, the cancer is gone, but the damage remains.

The follow-up CT scan of my lungs shows the cancer nodules are continuing to grow. My doctor is concerned that if I continue to do nothing (no treatment), in a few more months my chest pain and breathing issues will worsen beyond any help. She told me of one of her current patients who also has metastatic ACC in her lungs and whose symptoms are worse than mine. After just three months of

ed for a season or two, hoping and praying the grass would overcome the weeds. But that didn't happen.

Then I tried a few highly targeted "weed extracts" aimed at killing the roots while not harming the grass. These were also ineffective.

So now, I am faced with the choice of spraying the entire lawn (and surrounding landscape) with highly toxic weed killer. The hope is this will reduce some of the weeds and slow their growth without damaging the grass or other

My lungs are like a well-manicured lawn with weeds sprouting up in the grass. Unfortunately, there are too many weeds to pull out one-by-one.

chemo, the tumors shrunk and her symptoms went away.

My doctor also has another patient with a situation similar to mine whose nodules shrunk with chemo, but started growing again after six months.

Chemo is not a cure.

But there's a better than 40% chance that my cancer nodules would shrink for at least some months. And I would feel better for a while longer. The goal is to give me more time to find additional clinical trials. I've already done three trials that didn't work and am currently in line for two others in various cities. But they are not open at this time. I'm praying about and pondering my next step and will decide after the upcoming throat surgery. I am relieved to hear this particular chemo is relatively easy. It won't make me sick or have hair loss. If it's a by-weekly infusion, I can still make some international trips.

If my suffering and pain and ultimately, my death can help move another person closer to knowing the love and grace of our God, so be it. It is well with my soul.

|||||||||||||||||||||||||||||||||||||||||||||||||||||||||

plant life too much. So that's the deal.

Please pray for me as I take these next steps. God remains my hope, my rock and my strong tower. He is sovereign, which means, HE is in control. Not me, not the doctors and not even the cancer. No matter what happens, I am in His hands. And if my suffering and pain and, ultimately, my death can help move another person closer to knowing the love and grace of our God, so be it. It is well with my soul.

Less
Is More

January 17, 2020

Less is more. You've heard the phrase. But here's what I'm learning about it these days. I'm learning to let go; not because the things I was clinging to were bad but because they had become a distraction. For over 25 years, I had planned to retire "early" and travel near and far offering support and help to Christian charities. I had NO IDEA that my retirement plan would really kick off while I was still working full time. This made it possible for a smooth transition from President/CEO of Brewer Direct to running my own charitable foundation where I spend time and energy doing exactly what I dreamed all those years ago.

When I sold my 100% ownership of my company (to the employees) some wondered if I had lost my mind. When I

MEDICAL UPDATE * Surgery was a success. I am breathing so much better and immediately got more energy and focus. I pray that this time around my throat remains open! I do have a sore throat and my voice is all but a whisper. These things were expected and should improve over time.

I also told my City of Hope doctor to start the chemo schedule.

returned my leased BMW and kept only the Porsche, people thought I'd miss having a second car. I recruited and hired my replacement at the agency, emptied my office and walked away from Brewer Direct, the company I started 15 years ago. People figured I'd be sorry.

More recently it was suggested I'd be emotional when I boxed up my personal belongings in Monrovia, moved out and put my 30-year home on the market. I was! I was overjoyed and not because any of these things were bad. It's just, as I let them go, I felt a weight was being lifted. Moving my Monrovia belongings to Seal Beach (now my primary residence) required shredding, donating and tossing nearly half of all the stuff I had hoarded for 58 years. What a blast to let it all go.

Moving my Monrovia belongings to Seal Beach (now my primary residence) required shredding, donating and tossing nearly half of all the stuff I had hoarded for 58 years. What a blast to let it all go.

Please pray that this shrinks the tumors in my lungs with minimum side effects. And remember also to pray that my healing, which was bought and paid for on the cross, will be fully realized "on earth as it is in heaven." That is my desire and confession. Nevertheless, my hope is in Him alone.

*My job, car and house and all
my belongings were not sin. No way.
But they had become weights.
Distractions in the race God
has set before me.*

||||||||||||||||||||||||||||||||||||||||||||||

Hebrews 12:1 says, "Therefore, since we are surrounded by so great a cloud of witnesses, let us also lay aside every weight, and sin which clings so closely, and let us run with endurance the race that is set before us."

I feel lighter. I feel freer. My job, car and house and all my belongings were not sin. No way. But they had become weights. Distractions in the race God has set before me. The race God called me to over 25 years ago. Now I can run free. I wonder where I'll be running to next?

Dark Week
of the Soul

February 2, 2020

W e sing the chorus, "Good Father" in church. "You're a good, good father, it's who you are, it's who you are. And I am loved by you. It's who I am, It's who I am." I reso- nate with the song because I didn't have a good relationship with my dad.

MEDICAL UPDATE ✴ In the 16th century, the Spanish mystic St. John of the Cross wrote a poem which later was given the title "Dark Night of the Soul." While it was not written as a response to life's challenges, many have defined it that way. The idea of a "dark night" referencing a spiritual crisis took hold in the Roman Catholic Church in the 19th century.

This week I experienced the darkest "night" I have had in years. I was taken low and felt completely abandoned by God. I'm generally mostly hopeful and upbeat, even as I struggle to live with a progres- sive and terminal disease; however, this week my body, soul and spirit came under assault like never before. It's been hard to remain hopeful.

Each new treatment I undergo leaves me with worse results. A few weeks ago, after breathing once again deteriorated, I scheduled a follow-up throat procedure. Only this time a little more aggressive. So far it has helped me breathe more freely. Unfortunately, it's left

I haven't been feeling the Father's goodness this week. On Saturday morning, I woke up to a text message from Martin of the Anointed Crushers in Uganda. Unprompted, he wrote, "We are practicing a song with the choir for tomorrow's service. It's called "Good Father" by Chris Tomlin." The song was new for them, and he and I had never discussed it before. Just twelve hours earlier I had written the "Good Father" lyrics on a draft version of this blog post, followed by my response. "How are you a good Father,

In those few moments God spoke to my feelings of abandonment with a gentle reminder of who He is... a good, good father.

||||||||||||||||||||||||||||||||||||||||||||||||||

me nearly voiceless, which I fear will be permanent. For a natural communicator like me, to be stricken mute is a severe blow. I can whisper, but am unable to have a conversation by phone or in any public space such as at a coffee shop, church, basketball game or even in a moving car.

A week ago I finally decided to start the "easy" chemo treatment plan of weekly infusions, which will last several months. I was promised minimal side effects with a good chance to shrink the tumors in my lungs, reduce my chest pain and extend my life. After just one treatment and a day or two of typical nausea and fatigue, I was doubled over, writhing in so much pain that I went to the emergency room, twice, for over 16 hours. I was admitted to the hospital overnight for treatment related to a "rare" side effect from the chemo drugs.

I have never experienced this level of ongoing intense pain. It has been physically and morally crushing.

watching me suffer and doing nothing?"

Martin's text was God's response. I don't believe in coincidences! This was an invasion into my pity party, God's personal way of saying, "Yes, Randy, you do have a good, good father. Even if you feel differently, it doesn't change the fact." In those few moments God spoke to my feelings of abandonment with a gentle reminder of who He is...a good, good father.

"For you did not receive the spirit of slavery to fall back into fear, but you have received the spirit of adoption as sons, by whom we cry, "Abba! Father!" (Rom. 8:15).

"Oh, taste and see that the Lord is good! Blessed is the man who takes refuge in Him!" (Ps. 34:8).

This divine "reset" has helped put me on the mend from this week's physical challenges. And I have called off chemo for the foreseeable future. It's time to live a quality of life over quantity. I plan to visit a pain management doctor in a few weeks for recommendations for my growing chest pains. I'll also follow up with my throat doctor. If my voice does not improve I'll need to consider options. I live with the ongoing tension of knowing I need to accept what is, as God's plan for my life, while also fighting things that are not in God's plan. And believing that none of this precludes God's sovereignty.

The apostle Paul wrote in 2 Timothy 4:7-8, "I have fought the good fight, I have finished the race, I have kept the faith. Henceforth there is laid up for me the crown of righteousness, which the Lord, the righteous judge, will award to me on that day, and not only to me but also to all who have

*Paul recognized his time was short
but also knew that he had finished
the race. Someone else could continue
to run the race.*

|||||||||||||||||||||||||||||||||||||||||||||||||||

loved his appearing." Paul recognized his time was short but also knew he had finished the race. Someone else would continue to run the race. Paul had "fought, finished and kept"—all past tense verbs. He could, therefore, look forward to the crown of righteousness.

Tradition tells us Paul was beheaded as a martyr in Rome by the emperor Nero approximately two years after he wrote his letter to Timothy. I am not yet at the finish line of my race. I am still fighting the good fight, running the race, keeping the faith. I'm not yet ready for my crown.

I've spoken before about the Texas-based band, Carrollton. This morning I listened to their song "In-Between" from the album *Everything or Nothing.* I conclude with the lyrics of "In-Between"©

*It's easy to praise Your name from the mountains
Or call on You from below
When everything's going right for me
Or I'm feeling alone
There have been times I have stood in victory
Or fallen in defeat
But most of my time is spent in the days
In the days in between*

You are the God for my days
I will trust in all Your ways
Take my hands and guide my feet
I know You're leading me
I'm gonna dance with You in the in between

I've been reading amazing stories
Of all the faithful ones
And wondering why every day
Doesn't look like that for me
Show me the miracles in the simple
Open my eyes to see
The beautiful life is found in the journey
In the days in between

You are the God for my days
I will trust in all Your ways
Take my hands and guide my feet
I know You're leading me
I'm gonna dance with You in the in between

I'm gonna dance
Gonna dance with You
Dance with You

You are the God for my days
I will trust in all Your ways
Take my hands and guide my feet

I know You're leading me
I'm gonna dance with You in the in between

Gonna dance, gonna dance with You
Every day in the in between

Dance, dance
Dance, dance[4]

How Are You Feeling?

February 29, 2020

Even in my worst moments I have tried to remain positive and hopeful. I have continually reached for life and lived it as best I can. However, during my recent physical downturn, I've begun thinking more about death. It's generally acknowledged that our top two fears are public speaking and death. I'm glad to say that neither are fears of mine.

MEDICAL UPDATE *

Several times a day I am asked, "How are you feeling?" Here's my answer. I have trouble breathing and I can barely talk. This is unlikely to improve. I cannot make phone calls, video calls or have public conversations. Please don't ask me to do so. It is too painful physically and crushes me emotionally.

But still I seek remedies. I am scheduled for speech therapy and I am also considering a series of PRP (platelet-rich plasma) injections into my vocal cords. This is a new, trial procedure. I'm still doing research.

However, it's the cancer in my lungs that is truly troubling. I can't breathe without feeling pain in my chest and side, nearly unbearable at times. I have shortness of breath just walking from room to room. The cancerous tumors are growing. I continue to seek clinical trials. I have scheduled several rounds of chemo (reduced dose) with the hope it doesn't send me to the hospital like last time.

I still don't understand why God, my loving father, would ordain

Public speaking is certainly off the table for me. I can't talk, much less speak in public. As a Christian and a believer, I take assurance in 1 Corinthians 15:55-57:

> Death is swallowed up in victory. O death, where is your victory? O death, where is your sting? The sting of death is sin, and the power of sin is the law. But thanks be to God, who gives us the victory through our Lord Jesus Christ.

Sovereignty means that God doesn't just sit out when bad things happen, He is ultimately in charge, after all, He is God, right? And that's what is so hard for me to accept.

these steps for me. It's a grueling race God has me running. Every step is sheer pain. People are now calling me Job. It sort of feels appropriate.

The suffering is relentless and worsening. Even the little things I used to enjoy, like eating out with friends, going to Laker games, to name a few, are being taken away from me. If I am going to identify with Job, I can't edit the text to fit my situation. I have to read and receive all of it.

"Shall we receive good from God, and shall we not receive evil?" Job asks. Let's not argue whether God is responsible for evil. That's a nonstarter. But God is sovereign which means that He doesn't just sit out when bad things happen. He is ultimately in charge. That's why suffering is so hard for me to accept. I don't believe life is random and without purpose. But my relentless suffering leaves me very angry. I don't see the good in it.

Even those whom Jesus raised from the dead later died again. As did everyone He healed. All of them! For our lives to be fully restored, we must first die.

ıı

Except for Enoch and Elijah, death is inevitable and unavoidable. Death is, in point of fact, the only thing that all of us have in common. Yet, we push it away and try to ignore it. Many people fear death because they fear the unknown. Scripture addresses this fear when it tells us that to be absent from the body is to be present with the Lord (2 Cor. 5:8).

Death is not unknown at all. It is being present with the Lord who knows us and loves us. But that doesn't mean death is not tragic, and dying not hard. Especially when the process literally destroys the body, as my cancer is doing.

Death is a fundamental reality of life, yet still a mystery. As are the things that cause death, like my disease. There is no timetable for death. No one can tell me when I will die. And few have anything to say about how the growing cancer will feel and in what ways it will debilitate me.

Let me say emphatically, God is able to miraculously heal my body. More than that, He can raise me from the dead, if He chooses. Jesus raised at least three people from the dead that we know about. Knowing this, I continue to pray for a miraculous restoration to good health, and I wait with hope (eager expectation) that God will do it. I treasure your agreement with me in this prayer.

But I also know my true healing will not take place on

earth. Even those whom Jesus raised from the dead later died again. As did everyone He healed. All of them!

For our lives to be fully restored, we must first die. The deepest miracle is not restoring life to a dead person, alive again in the same body. The real miracle is eternal life in a new body that will never wear out or be destroyed. This was God's purpose for us from the beginning. A purpose He accomplished by sending His son to die on a cross to purchase our forgiveness, making us spiritually whole and granting us eternal life in His presence…for those who believe.

It's a balancing act. On one hand my physical condition, pain and suffering anger me and leave me with questions. I am unsure how much more I can handle.

But my faith in God and His sovereignty and the work of Jesus on the cross hasn't wavered. In fact, being angry is an expression of faith. If it weren't for my faith, I am not sure I would still be alive. Faith has given me an anchor of hope in the midst of the storm. A line from the song "I Will Fear No More" by The Afters comes to mind: "Even though I'm in the storm, the storm is not in me."

That's the balance. I feel every bit of the raging storm beating against me. It hurts! But deep inside, there is a calm. I don't always exhibit it. Sometimes I let the storm get to me. But the calm is there—always. Thank God.

I had the good pleasure of knowing a prolific Christian songwriter and artist in my earlier years. His name was Dave De Coup-Crank. Really, that was his name. Unfortunately, he died of cancer at age 52. One of his many songs touched me deeply many years ago, and is being renewed in my spirit again today.

Death Before Life©

I guess you heard what happened on the radio today,
but you could not believe it you were with me yesterday.
And now my life is closing like a flower in the night,
and the battle still is raging, but I'm giving up the fight.
And I'm leaving the darkness and moving into the light.
You know I used to wonder why I was here,
when I tried to face eternity, I closed my eyes with fear.
You see I'm bound here by the chains of life,
but my freedom's coming near.
I'm shackled and bound,
but when the trumpet sounds,
I'm bound to be free, no more misery, I'm bound to be free,
so do not cry for me, because I'm bound to be free,
I'm bound to be free.[5]

What Does It Mean to Trust?

March 10, 2020

Some trust in chariots and some in horses, but we trust in the name of the Lord our God" (Prov. 20:7).

It boils down to trust. Leaning on God. Praying and listening. Yes, I asked family and friends for their thoughts.

MEDICAL UPDATE *

Do you know the "Trust Fall"? It's an object lesson to teach trust among a group of people, and involves one person falling back into the arms of another. But trust in God is much deeper than that.

"Trust in the Lord with all your heart, and do not lean on your own understanding. In all your ways acknowledge him, and he will make straight your paths" (Prov. 3:5-6).

This can be hard to understand. Does trust mean we are to set our minds aside and not pursue any rational analysis? I don't think so. Consider the word *lean*. When we lean, we put our weight on what we are leaning on.

This scripture doesn't discourage thinking, only that we should not overly rely on our own thinking. That's why the text follows with, "in ALL your ways acknowledge him." Trusting in God means putting all your weight and reliance on Him. We can think through things. We can analyze and give consideration, but ultimately, we must lean on God.

My own illness is a case study in trust. I sought counsel. I worked through the pros and cons and created a virtual rubric to evaluate options. And do all humanly possible. But ultimately, it came down to

I also asked for friends to pray that God would speak to me. And He did, late on Sunday night and then again early Monday morning. I felt a peace that only God can give.

"All the days ordained for me were written in your book before one of them came to be" (Prov. 139:16).

God has me covered. I am grateful for the medical help I have received. I believe God uses medicine and health-care to heal. But no amount of medicine or healthcare will advance my days beyond what God has ordained for me. I need to lean on that truth.

And I continue to pursue medical options. I head to Boston in early April to consult with a cancer institute that has a clinical trial aimed at being a cure, not just a stop-gap. So far it hasn't made anyone sick or have weird side-effects. I

---

spending an evening in prayer, searching the scripture and gaining confirmation as God spoke to me with His still small voice as only He does.

The last time I tried chemo, I ended up in the hospital. Then last week, after consultation with two doctors, I went for it again, using a slightly lower chemo dose. Once again, I was hit with a series of "very rare" side effects that had me at CVS every day for a week, picking up meds. I had a decision to make.

Unlike most cancers, mine cannot be cured through chemo. The best I can hope for is slowing the cancer enough to give me a few more months. The trade-off, however, is costly. Chemo would force me to give up most of what I can still enjoy: eating out with friends, going to a Lakers game, attending church and even taking walks on the beach. And I would continue to suffer the side effects: I'd feel terrible with flu-like symptoms plus other side-effects for as much as four or five months. That's a guarantee. Doctors want me to continue chemo. I understand their thinking.

We can think through things.
We can analyze and give consideration,
but at the end of the day,
we must lean on God.

IIIIIIIIIIIIIIIIIIIIIIIIIIIIIIIIIIIIIIIIIIIIIIIIIIII

am investigating this, and continuing to pray and trust God.

None of this has made my life easier, and I am forced to make hard decisions. I lean on God. I will trust. A song from Carrollton, which I've shared before, is fitting again today.

I Will Trust ©

Though the arrows fly
Though the terrors rage
Though there be no answers for the prayers I've prayed

I will trust
I will trust
I will trust in You

When I face the pain
That is sure to come
When deep sorrow rolls like waves I can't outrun

I will trust
I will trust
I will trust in You

You're my refuge
And my defense
How You love me I will trust
You're my fortress
And You're my strength
Oh, how You love me I will trust
You're my refuge
And my defense
How You love me I will trust
You're my fortress
And You're my strength
Oh, how You love me I will trust

I will trust
I will trust
I will trust in You
I will trust
I will trust
I will trust in You[2]

Who Moved My Peace?

April 8, 2020

In the early 2000s, the book *Who Moved My Cheese?* by Spencer Johnson was popular among businesses seeking to adapt to work or life change. The book, which read like a children's fable, sold over 26 million copies in 37 languages and remains a business best-seller. I continue to draw inspiration from the lessons learned in this book as I have pivoted from full-time business owner and CEO to semi-retired, charitable foundation leader.

However, the question I am asking today is not "Who moved my cheese?" It's, "Who moved my peace?"

As I've wrestled with a terminal cancer, I've been frequently complimented for exhibiting "great faith," "hope"

MEDICAL UPDATE ∗   I've been looking forward to traveling to Boston to learn more about a new clinical trial. However, with Coronavirus surging, I had to settle for a telemedicine consult with the doctor in Boston. He had looked at all my test results, and the consult was the most encouraging I've had in months. The doctor and his team specialize in ACC and have been successfully treating numerous patients with the disease. After going over my medical history, current health, and

and "peace." Some believe I will beat the odds. "Randy? He'll live forever," they say. "Yes, with Jesus," I respond.

But I have proved to be durable. I'm like one of those cowboys in an old "spaghetti western" who gets shot multiple times, falls over, coughs blood, and miraculously gets up to keep on fighting. That's me for these past eight years. My faith and peace have been shaken, but I've grown accustomed to the ups and downs of this condition. I have learned to trust in the sovereign nature of God who numbered my days even before I was born.

So why have I felt such anxiety of late? Why am I not experiencing the "peace that surpasses all understanding" that the Bible promises?

God tells us not to worry because He knows it is our nature to worry, especially when we face unknown danger. The COVID-19 pandemic is one such danger worrying me.

I'm like one of those cowboys in an old "spaghetti western" who gets shot multiple times, falls over, coughs blood and miraculously gets up to keep on fighting.

recent treatments, we agreed that a new clinical trial could start via telemedicine. A daily low-dose of some pills which have no significant side-effects. We don't know if it will be effective. Please pray.

The doctor was positive about my prognosis. I still have a lot of healthy lung, and my tumor biopsy revealed my rare cancer is also very slow growing. After I complete an online consent, and get a local CT scan, they will mail me the pills. Thank you, God!

How long will the lockdown last? How many will die? Will a vaccine or treatment be discovered? Will I get it? Will the economy recover?

Questions keep piling, but no answers are coming from the President, CDC, our Governor or medical personnel. No wonder my peace is shaken.

When I feel like this, I turn to Scripture. Apostle Paul writes in Philippians 4:6-9:

> Do not be anxious about anything, but in everything by prayer and supplication with thanksgiving let your requests be made known to God. And the peace of God, which surpasses all understanding, will guard your hearts and your minds in Christ Jesus. Finally, brothers, whatever is true, whatever is honorable, whatever is just, whatever is pure, whatever is lovely, whatever is commendable, if there is any excellence, if there is anything worthy of praise, think about these things. What you have learned and received and heard and seen in me—practice these things, and the God of peace will be with you.

Paul says do not be anxious about anything. Paul understands anxiety to be a choice. We can choose to not give ourselves over to anxiety, and we can instead pray, and ask God to intervene in our worries and thank Him, in advance, for His answer. That's the anti-anxiety prescription from the Bible.

But Paul doesn't stop there. Once we've chosen not to be anxious, we can choose what to set our minds on. Paul uses

*Did you realize, being anxious is
a choice? ...We can choose to give
ourselves to anxiety or we can instead,
pray, ask God to intervene in our
worries and then thank Him, in advance,
for how He will answer.*

eight different adjectives to describe what should fill our minds. When we practice them, God's peace will be with us.

I realized my peace had been replaced by anxiety because I had chosen to meditate on the wrong things. Throughout this pandemic I have become glued to the media. It started innocently. I just wanted to know the latest, important recommendations, which the media furiously spins out to keep viewers tuned in.

The more I watched the more anxious I became. I began to imagine I had the virus. Every sniffle or cough was a sign. I was doomed. The news confirmed it. And then it dawned on me. I could stop being anxious simply by turning off the news and spending more time filling my mind with scripture, online sermons, encouraging readings, and worship or praise music. Even comedy TV shows. Something to put my mind and heart in the right place. That was my way back to peace.

Are you wondering who moved your peace? The answer may be you. And it's easy to get your peace back. God is not in short supply. Simply change your focus. Choose not to be anxious, and instead pray. Fill your mind with good things, whatever they may be. For me, it's God's word. What could be better than that?

I close with a song that has recently inspired me by Switch, featuring Dillan Chase.

Symphony[©]

Sometimes it's hard to breathe
All these thoughts they shout at me
Try to bring me to my knees
And it's overwhelming
Darkness echoes all around
Feels like everything is crashing down
Still I know where my hope is found
And it's only you and ooh-ooh

You say you're working everything for my good and ooh-ooh
I believe every word
'Cause even in the madness
There is peace
Drownin' out the voices
All around me
Through all of this chaos
You are writing a symphony
A symphony
And even in the madness
There is peace
Drownin' out the voices
All around me
Through all of this chaos

You are writing a symphony
A symphony, oh

Tune my heart to your beat
Let me be your melody
Even when I cannot see
But you orchestrate it
Even when the dark surrounds
You'll never let me drown
I know that my hope is found
In the name of Jesus, Ooh-ooh

You say you're working everything for my good
And ooh-ooh
I believe every word
'Cause even in the madness
There is peace
Drownin' out the voices
All around me
Through all of this chaos
You are writing a symphony
A symphony
And even in the madness
There is peace
Drownin' out the voices
All around me
Through all of this chaos
You are writing a symphony
A symphony, oh

Yo, I wanna truly know
If you compose beautiful
Music, though
From all my unruly notes
Distance is distant, it's movin' close
Now I see, erase the scales from my eyes
Then play the scale of my life
Chaos played off with a chord in accord
With a source prevailing through strife and

I've tasted suffering
I've been embraced by the painful buffering
I've been bound by doubts so loud right now
But a melody is made when you play these rusty keys
So we all gotta get pressed
Tuned up like instruments
But I know
All of life's tempo is set
Whenever we remember this

That even in the madness
There is peace
Drownin' out the voices
All around me
Through all of this chaos
You are writing a symphony
A symphony
And even in the madness
There is peace

Drownin' out the voices
All around me
Through all of this chaos
You are writing a symphony
A symphony, oh
Ooh-oh-oh, ooh-oh-oh, ooh-oh-oh, a symphony[6]

The Middle
of a Miracle

May 12, 2020

E xodus 14 describes the events of Moses leading the
people of Israel through the Red Sea. They were being
chased by Pharaoh and his army who wanted to bring them
back into slavery in Egypt. What a scene. Behind them,
Pharaoh, his soldiers, and 600 chariots in hot pursuit. And
in front of them, the daunting Red Sea. It's no wonder they
feared for their lives and cried out to Moses that it would
have been better for them to have stayed in Egypt as slaves.
Hadn't God already done miracle after miracle to deliver

MEDICAL UPDATE *

The day after I had been accepted into a new promising clinical drug trial in Boston, I got the call to come to Boston for a full
day of medical tests.

It was scheduled in the middle of the Coronavirus surge in Mas-
sachusetts, April 22-23. However, everything went perfectly, thank
God. I began the new medication (nine relatively small pills per day)
on Monday, April 27, and the side-effects have been minor and manageable. I will continue taking the meds for another two weeks (one
month in all), get a blood test locally and touch base with my Boston
doctor via Zoom.

If all goes well, I'll continue taking the medication for a second

them? Apparently, God was only as good as His last miracle, which didn't guarantee another.

Moses wasn't having any of it. He said, "Fear not, stand firm and see the salvation of the Lord, which he will work for you today. For the Egyptians whom you see today, you shall never see again. The Lord will fight for you, and you only have to be silent" (Exod. 14:13-14, ESV).

I love that. In essence, Moses, ever short of fuse, yelled, "Shut up and let God work!" I wonder how many times God has wanted to say the same to us...to me?

Of course, you know the rest of the story. But put yourself there for a moment. You are milling with millions of Israelis on the banks of the Red Sea when suddenly a tunnel of hurricane force east wind starts to whip up the water, then forms a wall on either side while drying out the mud on the seabed.

Moses has already formed all Israel and their animals into regiments to walk across the seabed, while the winds rage and the walls of water hold. Can you imagine the noise

---

month and follow with a CT scan to determine if the medication has shrunk the tumors in my lungs.

I continue to ask God for a miracle. I feel well, generally. I've had some voice therapy to eke out some improvement in speaking and breathing. I try to exercise daily. I've exhausted much of Netflix, HBO GO, Amazon Prime. I am eager to see friends in person, and I don't feel especially vulnerable. Although I had no symptoms, I took the COVID-19 test just before traveling to Boston to put my mind at ease. The results were negative, as expected. It's been more than 14 days since my trip. I still have no symptoms so I remain Coronavirus-free.

*Let's celebrate what He is doing
even if there seems to be enemies
chasing us and walls of water
on the left and the right.*

and the chaos? The terror of that march?

I'd be running for my life, maybe in circles. Or maybe I'd be frozen in fear, afraid of the water crashing down on me. Or running the other direction, taking my chances with Pharaoh. The Bible is largely silent about that all-night journey through the Red Sea. It gives us the big picture but skips the details. I wonder, if I were there in the midst of a miracle, might I have missed it? Would I have let my anxiety and fear so consume my mind and heart that God's mighty hand of deliverance would (once again) go unheralded?

There is always a Pharaoh. For me, it's the terminal cancer. And all of us are being pursued by a common enemy in COVID-19. The virus is relentless. Death and heartache are real. Many have been in quarantine for weeks on end. The economies of the world, especially the US, are on shaky ground. There remains a fragile recovery process for our nation. The future is unknown.

But in all of it, I'm reminded of what God said to the people of Israel: "Fear not, stand firm, and see the salvation of the Lord, which He will work for you today. For the Egyptians (insert your enemy here...cancer, COVID-19, economy, etc.) whom you see today, you shall never see again.

The Lord will fight for you, and you have only to be silent" (Exodus 14:13-14).

We are crossing the Red Sea right now, on dry ground… in the middle of a miracle. Let's celebrate what He is doing even as our enemies chase us and walls of water rise over us on the left and the right. God is bringing us to safety on the other side. Praise God for His deliverance. Let's not miss what God is doing.

But It Still Burns!

May 26, 2020

I continue to process the ongoing suffering brought about by my cancer and our efforts to fight it. If you've followed my blog at all, you know that I go through valleys of suffering and despair along with the peaks of learning and growth. It is an amazing journey I would have never chosen.

I think about people like Ravi Zacharias, the author, speaker and Christian apologist who died within months of being diagnosed with cancer when seeking remedy for

MEDICAL UPDATE * I returned from Boston on April 23. On April 27 I began the nine pill 90 mg per day regimen of ATRA, widely used for other cancers but only now being tested for metastatic ACC. For nearly three weeks I dosed morning and night with only minor side-effects. In the middle of my third week I got a sore throat. Not the type of sore throat that indicates a cold but more of a swollen throat. I tried to sleep it off but it got worse.

After the usual home remedies didn't help, I spoke to the doctor and we agreed to "hold" the trial drug for a few days to see if things would subside. Unfortunately, things didn't improve. It became extremely difficult and painful to swallow so I made an urgent appointment with my throat doctor at USC.

back pain. What a gifted communicator he was. His voice in Christendom will be missed. He suffered for a season, and I am going on eight years!

Why has God chosen this road for me?

One possible reason: He is using this journey to purify me. Hebrews 12:11 reads: "For the moment all discipline seems painful rather than pleasant, but later it yields the peaceful fruit of righteousness to those who have been trained by it."

Before the theologians crucify me, I offer a caveat. I'm not saying God gave me cancer to discipline me. What father, wanting to correct their child, would give them a terminal illness? Matthew 7:11 specifically says that our Heavenly

How I view my relationship to God has changed my relationship with the things of this world. I don't need to prove myself to God, so I don't need to work so hard.

On May 19, a throat scope revealed Mucositis, a painful throat condition that is a frequent by-product of cancer drugs. The throat swelling will continue as long as I am on ATRA. So once again I must adjust to find a sweet spot that makes the process tolerable.

My Boston doctor had me lower the daily ATRA to 70 mg (7 pills per day). After just three and a half days my throat pain (which hadn't fully gone away) spiked to its highest levels. It was evident that this trial drug will not leave my throat alone. I have cancelled the trial but will have a CT scan to see if the drug slowed the cancer. This is the nature of a disease that has no known cure. We seek and try new unproven treatments, all of which have side-effects. Please continue to pray for me as I decide next steps.

For eight years, I've been put through the fire. Sometimes it feels like the heat is turned up to something I can't possibly handle.

Father gives us good gifts when we ask. What I am saying and firmly believe is that I know "that for those who love God all things work together for good, for those who are called according to his purpose" (Rom. 8:28).

It's not easy to piece all of this together. Suffering, along with the problem of evil, remains a mystery. Volumes have been written about the problem of suffering and the sovereignty of God. I can't begin to tackle any of that here.

All I can do is share openly and honestly about my own experience. Eight years ago, I was headed in one direction. I wasn't going astray, or being selfish. But I had plans. And I was living out those plans as I felt God was directing me. I also failed. A lot. And frankly, I still do.

Then came cancer in 2012, and my priorities changed. My life's plans came to a screeching halt. From the outside it might not have looked like anything had changed. I had lived honestly and had hopes of giving my life away in some form of retirement. I spent a lot of time with friends and tried to be a good mentor and good example of faithful living. I messed up plenty. My life today might seem much the same. But I know differently.

The author of Hebrews tells us that discipline produces

the peaceful fruit of righteousness. Bad things in our lives are generally not a means of discipline, but God can still do the same, and help produce the peaceful fruit of righteousness from bad things in our lives. The simple definition of righteousness is "right living." Therefore, the fruit of righteousness is the product of a life lived rightly, the result of which is peace.

Eight years ago, I was busy building a business, growing my wealth and amassing stuff (two homes, vacation home in Florida, two cars, etc.). None of this was a bad thing. I employed dozens of people. My company helped thousands of needy people around the country. But today, things that once meant a lot to me don't matter so much. How I view my relationship to God has changed my relationship with the things of this world. I don't need to prove myself to God, so I don't need to work so hard. I'm at peace with God's plan for me and find my days less busy, less complicated, yet much more satisfying.

The Bible depicts the purification process as gold being placed in the fire. The intense heat melts the gold and sends the impurities, the dross, to the surface to be removed.

That is what I am experiencing. For eight years, I've been put through the fire. Sometimes it feels like the heat will consume me. But God is using it to produce the peaceful fruit of righteousness in me. Job said: "But he knows the way that I take; when he has tried me, I shall come out as gold" (Job 23:10, ESV). Job knew what I am still learning. God is making me pure gold. But it still burns!

I was thinking of this old chorus from 2004.

Refiner's Fire ©

Purify my heart
Let me be as gold and precious silver
Purify my heart
Let me be as gold, pure gold
Refiner's fire
My heart's one desire
Is to be holy
Set apart for You, Lord
I choose to be holy
Set apart for You, my Master
Ready to do Your will
Purify my heart
Cleanse me from within
And make me holy
Purify my heart
Cleanse me from my sin
Deep within[7]

By Brian Doerksen

Inside the Fires of Sorrow!

June 27, 2020

There aren't enough books on the theology of suffering. As a charismatic Christian who believes in healing (see Isa. 53: 5, Matt. 8:14-17, 1 Pet. 2:24), I choose to believe that

MEDICAL UPDATE * This is a tough post to write. I promised to be honest and share the story unvarnished.

I recently wrote about my latest clinical trial drug called ATRA and the unfortunate side-effects in my throat (Mucositis), which caused me to stop it early. This was my fourth targeted drug trial.

The first one was considered immunotherapy, the second a gene inhibitor and the two others were oral chemo. None of them slowed the growth of the tumors in my lungs. They only compounded my problems by causing medical conditions that I'm still dealing with. I also tried traditional chemotherapy twice. Both times I ended up in the emergency room, and once in the hospital for an overnight treatment of a painful side-effect called Ileus.

A CT scan on June 13th showed the cancer still growing. My lungs are now 50% blocked by ACC tumors. The doctors figure, at this rate, I'll need full-time oxygen in six to 12 months. No one talks about the end of my life, but I can do the math. At the current growth rate (tumor size doubling every two years) I project my lungs will be completely blocked in 18-24 months when I will no longer be able to breathe.

People have asked about the possibility of double lung transplants, (impossible for cancer patients) as well as other various treatments they've read or heard about. Trust me, I have pursued everything. I was just offered yet another new drug trial with known side-effects.

God wants His children to be whole and healthy. After all, isn't that part of what Jesus accomplished at the cross, our redemption from sin and death as well as the healing from sickness and disease? However, Christians still get sick and die, every day as they did throughout biblical times. These experiences are not outside God's sovereignty. We could use more books on this subject from good, spirit-filled theologically sound scholars. I hope that changes.

Until then, I give you this blog post.

I believe we put too much emphasis on our lives here on earth which are but a "puff of smoke" (James 4:14). Jesus tells us not to get caught up with temporary things

---

I turned it down. Doctors have yet again recommended a regimen of chemotherapy, this one four months. Again, I have said no. Both could possibly extend my life a year or more. But neither is a cure. So, I just can't do it, at least not now.

Listen closely. People see me as a man of big faith. I'm not. I am a man of mustard seed sized faith in a big God. He can do what medicine has failed to do.

I'm not saying medicine is bad or ungodly. I wrote an entire book, *Finding My Voice*, about my first miracle surgery. I thank God for modern medicine and all God does through doctors. All of us have to accept that God has our days numbered and all the medicine in the world won't add a minute to our life beyond what He has ordained. God is sovereign and He remains on the throne.

Don't get me wrong, I have not thrown in the towel. God has also instructed us to number our days (Ps. 90:12.) I want to live, and I continue praying for a #HezekiahMiracle. (Read about this in 2 Kings 20:1, 2 Chron. 32:24 and Isa. 38:1.) At the end of my second book, *Releasing Generosity*, I outlined my goal for the end of my life with three initials O.B.E. I want to end my life Old, Broke and Exhausted. In two months I'll be 59, and that's not old. I still have some money left and a lot of energy. So, I have some work left to do to. Pray that God grants me a #HezekiahMiracle so I can end my life #OBE.

In the end, cancer, disease, suffering of any kind, even death is a momentary affliction because these are things seen, transient and temporary. God has something eternal and far more glorious for us.

(Matthew 10:28, Matthew 6:34). Yes, we do begin to enjoy the benefits of Jesus' victory over death while we live on this earth, but the fulfillment of Jesus' finished work on the cross will not be realized until we are raised from the dead in a resurrection like his.

2 Corinthians 4:17-18 (ESV) helps me put it into perspective. I hope these verses will also help you:

> For this light momentary affliction is preparing for us an eternal weight of glory beyond all comparison, as we look not to the things that are seen but to the things that are unseen. For the things that are seen are transient, but the things that are unseen are eternal.

In the end, cancer, disease, suffering and death are momentary afflictions because our earthly lives are transient and temporary. Suffering is not meaningless, for it yields the eternal reward of a life lived with God. Suffering is used by God to prepare us for an "eternal weight of glory beyond all comparison." One of my favorite authors, Oswald Chambers, wrote, "If you receive yourself in the fires of sorrow, God will make you nourishment for others."

If I were to write a book about suffering, healing and God's sovereignty, I'd wrestle with the biblical promises of long life and the clear scriptural support for health and prosperity on earth as it is in heaven.

Yet, these promises are given within the context of the human condition, and our death as the final reality of life on earth. It's not as simple as saying "God wants all Christians to live to be 70 or 80" (Psa. 90:10) or he wants everyone to live free of any sickness (Deut. 7:12-15) or rich and prosperous (Jer. 29:11). It's holding in tension what theologians describe as the already and the not yet.

The "already" is the foretaste on earth of what we will experience in heaven. We don't get to have the fulness of heaven on earth. The "not yet" is what we long for, the fulfillment of every God given desire we have on earth. The promise of heaven to me will start with this: I will get a new set of lungs. But first I'll have to stop breathing.

Even so, I pray for God's healing and blessings to be experienced here and now. When I don't get what I pray for, I still trust God. Like Jesus, I hold my desires and my will up to heaven and say, your will be done Lord! In whatever way God directs my path, like the Apostle Paul, I know how to be "abased or to abound" and remain content either way (Phil. 4:11-13). I pray for you also, that God would direct your steps. I pray you would be free from hardships and pain, suffering and diseases. But no matter what comes your way, my deepest desire is that you be conformed into the image of God.

Another great song by the group Carrollton:

Giving It All To You©

I'll take my whole world
Put it into Your hands
I'm so tired of my plans
I'm giving it all to You

Why am I holding on so tightly
To my world and all these plans of mine
Your ways are infinite
Mine are limited
You give life and I want to start living it
I will put my trust in You

I'll take my whole world
Put it into Your hands
I'm so tired of my plans
I'm giving it all to You
Lord, take my whole life
It is mine no longer
You have always been stronger
I'm giving it all to You

Why do I doubt the things You promised
When Your truth has never failed before
'Cause Your ways are infinite, mine are limited
You give life and I want to start living it
I will put my trust in You

I'll take my whole world
Put it into Your hands
I'm so tired of my plans
I'm giving it all to You
Lord, take my whole life
It is mine no longer
You have always been stronger
I'm giving it all to You

If it's not Your plan
I don't want it, I don't want it
Take my hand
I'll keep walking, I'll keep walking
If it's not Your plan
I don't want it, I don't want it
Take my hand
I'll keep walking, I'll keep walking, I'll keep walking

I'll take my whole world
Put it into Your hands
I'm so tired of my plans
I'm giving it all to You
Lord, take my whole life
It is mine no longer
You have always been stronger
I'm giving it all to You[8]

Acceptance and God's Sovereign Will

August 12, 2020

"**F**or the mountains may depart and the hills be removed, but my steadfast love shall not depart from you, and my covenant of peace shall not be removed,' says the Lord, who has compassion on you" (Isa. 54:10, ESV).

Most of us are familiar with the five stages of grief: denial, anger, bargaining, depression and acceptance. Many assume a person goes through these stages sequentially, starting with stage one and ending with stage five. But in reality, a person facing significant trauma can go back and

---

MEDICAL UPDATE *

My breathing has become shallower and more labored. Activities once easy for me, like walking to the end of the pier, take enormous effort. With every step my breath comes in gasps. I have begun to use my oxygen machine throughout the days and nights, though I don't yet need it 24/7. The clinical trials and chemotherapy have not slowed the growth of cancer in my lungs. At this point, only a miracle can do that. The cancer won't go away any other way.

My throat remains somewhat sore. Doctors think it could be

forth between stages, from denial to bargaining then back to denial and then depression and more denial and then anger. It's not one size fits all. The same goes for me, but I can definitely say I have experienced all five stages of grief since first learning I had cancer in March 2012.

Today I want to focus on acceptance. To describe what acceptance looks like for someone who has the faith in God to heal, I turn to three biblical characters. I've blogged about each of them, but taken together, I hope you'll see how each of these men of faith came to accept God's sovereign will during very difficult times in their lives.

The exemplar of Old Testament suffering is Job. He complained to God and contended his blamelessness with his friends for weeks as he suffered. He is laid low with physical and emotional agony, but only in the final chapter of his story is he brought to his knees in humility at the sovereignty of God (Job 42:1-6). Only after he accepted God's will over his own, did his life, family and business get restored.

The great Apostle Paul, author of three quarters of the New Testament, was challenged by a "messenger of Satan" or thorn in the flesh (2 Cor. 12:7-9). We aren't told what the

---

muscle tension from straining to speak. A steroid shot in the neck muscles doesn't appear to have helped, so we will schedule an MRI. Swallowing has also become difficult. I am considering an out-patient procedure to stretch out my esophagus, clear out my airway and insert Plasma Rich Platelets (PRP) into a vocal cord to see if I can get better vocal use. The challenges of speaking, breathing and swallowing are most apparent to my friends, but it's the lung cancer that's killing me.

thorn was, but we know Paul didn't like it and asked multiple times for God to remove it. But God did NOT. Did Paul lack faith? I don't think so! God told Paul to "deal with it" (my loose translation); Paul too came to accept God's will over his own.

The third character is Jesus! We see him praying fervently in the garden, to the point of sweating drops like blood, to avoid the horrors of crucifixion (Luke 22:44). The gospel of Matthew describes Jesus' agony. In Matthew 26:38-39 Jesus says, "My soul is very sorrowful, even unto death. My Father, if it be possible, let this cup pass from me, nevertheless, not as I will, but as you will." After a few exasperated exchanges with his disciples, Jesus prays again, "My Father, if this cup cannot pass unless I drink it, your will be done."

Jesus progresses from denial to bargaining before coming to the place of acceptance, in his second time of prayer. Jesus, the one and only son of God, didn't pray away his pain and suffering. He prayed his way into his final passion. Jesus' faith, strong enough to move mountains, was strong enough to submit to death on a hill called Golgotha. It wasn't that Jesus did not have God's attention. It wasn't that his Father didn't care. Prayer was submission to his Father's will.

And so it is with us. God will accomplish His purpose through our suffering, not despite it.

From the outset of my cancer, I've questioned God, asking if I deserved all this suffering, wondering if my sins outweighed God's grace. I have gotten angry and yelled at God, "How could you...given all I did for you?!!"

Acceptance doesn't mean I stop
seeking God's miraculous intervention.
It's just that I release my demand
on God, my expectation of Him
as if He is my personal genie.

I've tried bargaining with God. Maybe if I gave away more of my money, helped more people and confessed more sins, God might change His mind.

I've been anointed with oil and prayed over. Yet my body continues to break down.

I've cried, felt alone, lost and utterly abandoned by God.

And finally, I have come to a place of acceptance. At least for now.

Acceptance doesn't mean I stop seeking God's miraculous intervention. Instead, I release my control, my demands of God, my expectation of Him as my personal genie. Perhaps God will do to me what He did for Job: complete physical healing and restoration of all I have lost. Maybe God wants me weakened by this disease so that my weakness will reflect His strength and grace, like the Apostle Paul. Perhaps God has planned an early death for me, as He did with His son, my savior. A death will have far-reaching impact, even more than if I had lived another 30+ years.

I don't know. God knows. And His plans are perfect and will work out for my good as well as others. I accept His will over my own. I rest knowing that "God's got this." He loves me. He hears me. He knows my desires. I pray that my desires reflect His will as much as I can know it. I only want my life to please Him. I only want to accurately reflect the love of Jesus in my life and death.

Like Hezekiah, I ask God for more time. I've been asking God for this since 2012. I believe He has graciously granted my request up to this very day. I have been all over the world, established a charitable foundation and been introduced to ministries and people we've partnered with to expand God's kingdom.

All of this SINCE being diagnosed with cancer. I've written two books, spoken at churches and events and traveled to more than a dozen countries, all during my battle with cancer. Thank you, God. You HAVE granted me more than eight years to serve You. May I continue to serve You all the days of my life until You call me home.

Here's another great song by a group called Big Daddy Weave.

I Know©

You don't answer all my questions
But You hear me when I speak
You don't keep my heart from breakin'
But when it does, You weep with me

You're so close that I can feel You
When I've lost the words to pray
And though my eyes have never seen You
I've seen enough to say

Chorus:
I know that You are good
I know that You are kind
I know that You are so much more
Than what I leave behind
I know that I am loved
I know that I am safe
'Cause even in the fire, to live is Christ, to die is gain
I know that You are good

I don't understand the sorrow
But You're calm within the storm
Sometimes this weight is overwhelming
But I don't carry it alone

You're still close when I can't feel You
I don't have to be afraid
And though my eyes have never seen You
I've seen enough to say

Repeat Chorus:

On my darkest day
From my deepest pain
Through it all, my heart, will choose to sing Your praise[9]

The Valley of the Shadow of Death

September 27, 2020

The 23rd Psalm, often read at funerals, is one you may have memorized.

The Lord is my shepherd; I shall not want. He makes me lie down in green pastures. He leads me beside still waters. He restores my soul. He leads me in paths of righteousness for his name's sake. Even though I walk through the valley of the shadow of death, I will fear no evil, for you are with me; your rod and your staff, they comfort me. You prepare a table before me in the presence of my enemies; you anoint my head with oil; my cup overflows. Surely goodness and

---

MEDICAL UPDATE ✳ What can I say that you don't already know? I have cancer in my lungs and it's growing. My breathing is becoming more labored. Wearing a mask is especially hard. However, when people see me they typically say, "You look good," which can also be translated as, "You don't look sick!"

I have realized often it's the cancer treatments, the chemotherapy and radiation, that take the life out of cancer patients. Since I have chosen not to pursue these treatments, I look OK even while I struggle with the disease.

mercy shall follow me all the days of my life, and I shall dwell in the house of the LORD forever.

The Psalmist recounts God's PROVISION (I shall not want) His PROTECTION (your rod and your staff, they comfort me) and His PROMISE (you prepare a table before me). But I want to focus on the phrase "even though I walk through the valley of the shadow of death..."

Scholars have suggested numerous meanings. David, the shepherd, certainly would have understood the fear and anxiety of one of his sheep being lost and alone in a dark valley. Later, as he fled for his life from King Saul, David was literally in the valley of the shadow of death. Some scholars believe this was the valley known in Arabic as Wadi Qelt. Familiar to travelers between Jerusalem and Jericho, the valley is filled with jagged rocks, uneven paths and potential

*It has felt often that I am
in death's shadow, in awful pain,
struggling to catch my breath.*

When I'm asked, "How are you doing?" I'm likely to answer, "I'm managing." That's because most of my attention these days is focused on managing the pain to limit my discomfort as best as possible. I appreciate your continued prayers for a miraculous healing. It isn't over 'til it's over. Please also pray that I endure through the pain and remain faithfully devoted to Jesus. One day I'll hear those words "Welcome home. Enter in my good and faithful servant."

On that day I'll have no more pain or suffering. But until that day, I am content to serve Him and "manage".

Perhaps that's why David wrote, I will fear no evil, for you are with me. He understood how scary the valley of death was... if he had been alone. But he was not alone. And neither am I.

||||||||||||||||||||||||||||||||||||||||||||||

threats from thieves (remember the Good Samaritan story from Luke 10?). But all agree, the valley of the shadow of death is synonymous with a place of peril, chaos, hardship and deep suffering. And that's exactly where I've been these past months—in death's shadow, in awful pain, struggling to breathe.

Once my brother-in-law, Ken, took me fishing at one of the local mountain lakes. We fished all day (I don't remember catching anything) and then set off on an evening hike. I followed closely as we climbed higher and higher up the hillside from the lakebed. As the sun set and the sky darkened, we turned around and had no idea where we were. Ken just thought it best to head downhill until we reached the lake.

With no light to see the path we tripped on loose rocks, fallen trees and I began to fall and slide in the dirt. I was anxious, holding back tears. I stayed very close to Ken for fear I might be left behind alone and lost. Ken eventually got us back to the lake, but not before I was covered in cuts and bruises.

It wasn't the valley of the shadow of death, but I was definitely scared to death. Perhaps that's why David wrote, I will fear no evil, for you are with me. He understood how scary the valley of death was… if he had been alone. But he was not alone. And neither am I. God is with me in this valley. I need not fear. Thank God for the comfort of His rod and staff (which I will discuss in another blog). Just as I stayed close to my brother-in-law Ken, I will remain close to Jesus and even when I fall, He promises to never leave me.

Music speaks to me on my journey. It always has. So many great songs. Here's one by Plumb. I hope it speaks to you too.

Need You Now[©]

Well, everybody's got a story to tell
And everybody's got a wound to be healed
I want to believe there's beauty here
'Cause oh, I get so tired of holding on
I can't let go, I can't move on
I want to believe there's meaning here

How many times have you heard me cry out
"God please take this"?
How many times have you given me strength to
Just keep breathing?
Oh I need you
God, I need you now.

Standing on a road I didn't plan
Wondering how I got to where I am
I'm trying to hear that still small voice
I'm trying to hear above the noise

How many times have you heard me cry out
God please take this?
How many times have you given me strength to
Just keep breathing?
Oh I need you
God, I need you now.

Though I walk,
Though I walk through the shadows
And I, I am so afraid
Please stay, please stay right beside me
With every single step I take

How many times have you heard me cry out?
And how many times have you given me strength?[10]

Almost Home

November 4, 2020

Psalm 139 is one of my favorites. David describes God's intimate knowledge of David even before he was born. What a comfort to David, and to us, to know the extent of God's personal involvement in his creation. In Psalm 138:8 David makes an amazing claim about God's plans for his life: "The Lord will fulfill his purpose for me; your steadfast love, O Lord, endures forever."

I recently turned 59 years old. By most standards, that's not old. 60 is the new 40! Unless you're stricken with terminal cancer at age 50. For 8½ years, cancer has plagued me and aged me. God has graciously used this time to further—if not completely—sanctify me. And He has allowed me to

MEDICAL UPDATE *   CT scans, an MRI and several throat scopes have failed to identify why I have ongoing throat pain. I was all set for a routine surgical procedure to clean out my throat, get some steroid shots (again) and even try a new PRP (Platelet Rich Plasma) shot, but I canceled. I just didn't feel good about being under general anesthetics again, especially with my breathing so shallow. Plus, the risk of another surgery to yield little benefit simply isn't worth it.

I am now using my O2 machine all the time. I am on a couple of meds

testify of His goodness and His sovereignty even through difficult situations. Please know I struggle through the first barrage of questions that emerge when bad things happen. Had my sin brought on my cancer? Did I lack the faith to see God heal it? Is my illness the work of the enemy? Should I denounce it and cast out the evil spirit of cancer?

Then I started to understand that God's ways truly are higher than mine.

I hadn't sinned my way to disease. The devil wasn't plaguing me with cancer. I have not stumbled into a dark alley with the devil or fallen out of favor with God.

Instead, I am exactly where God wants me. He has not left me. He is shaping Himself in me. I am sharing in His suffering, just a little. The creator of the universe and sovereign God has ordered every step, even these last few hard

I need not worry about the future.
I can rest knowing that no matter when
death comes, it will not be too soon
or too late. It will be right on time.

that help with pain and nausea. I am coming into this last phase of my disease with as much courage as I've ever had. Because I live alone, I recently initiated hospice services. Because I am no longer pursuing curative care (treatments for the disease), it is important that I have help with palliative care (management of pain and ease of suffering as my body fails me). I remain independent and do what I need to do—grocery shopping, lunches outside, etc.—but I'll have a nurse or supportive folks to check-in on me from time to time.

*Perhaps I hadn't sinned my way
to disease and the devil wasn't plaguing
me with cancer. Instead, I am exactly
where God wants me.*

ones. And His purpose is being fulfilled. I can't thwart it, and the devil can't stop it. Knowing this gives me peace. I need not worry about the future. I can rest knowing that no matter when death comes, it will not be too soon or too late. It will be right on time.

It's my hope and prayer that my journey, as captured here in real-time, draws you closer to Jesus. And if or when your own path takes a challenging turn, and it causes you to question God, go for it. He's up for honest questions. Just be ready for His answers. If your faith is stretched through adversity, good! That's your heavenly father forming Himself in you.

MercyMe sings a song called "Almost Home,"© which ministers to me at this time. Here are the lyrics.

*Are you disappointed
Are you desperate for help
You know what it's like to be tired
And only a shell of yourself
Well you start to believe
You don't have what it takes
Cause it's all you can do
Just to move much less finish the race*

But don't forget what lies ahead

Almost home
Brother it won't be long
Soon all your burdens will be gone
With all your strength
Sister run wild run free
Hold up your head
Keep pressing on
We are almost home

Well this road will be hard
But we win in the end
Simply because of Jesus and us
It's not if but when
So take joy in the journey
Even when it feels long
Oh find strength in each step
Knowing heaven is cheering you on

We are almost home
Brother it won't be long
Soon all your burdens will be gone
With all your strength
Sister run wild run free
Hold up your head
Keep pressing on
We are almost home
Almost home

Almost home

I know that the cross has brought heaven to us
But make no mistake there's still more to come
When our flesh and our bone are no longer between
Where we are right now and where we're meant to be
When all that's been lost has been made whole again
When these tears and this pain no longer exist
No more walking we're running as fast as we can
Consider this our second wind

Almost home
Brother it won't be long
Soon all your burdens will be gone
With all your strength
Sister run wild run free
Hold up your head
Keep pressing on
We are almost home
Almost home
Almost home
We are almost home
Almost home
Almost home
We are almost home[11]

Postscript

Fall 2020

One summer day in 1988, I remember picking up a CD from the Christian rock band Shout. It was their first record, so I opened it up and put it into my CD player with great anticipation. I skimmed the first couple of songs but then "It Won't Be Long" came on. I loved the opening guitar work, but then the 4-octave vocals of Ken Tamplin kicked in—and I loved it even more. What a great song. It rocks.

The song's message, simply put, is that the Lord is coming back soon, so as Christians, we need to share the gospel with anyone who will listen. And for everyone else, you need to get ready.

The gospel message is this. God is holy. We are not. After years attempting to reach God on our own, He finally sent His son, Jesus, to bridge the gap. Jesus did what no one else could do. He lived a perfect life yet sacrificed himself in order to open the way to God now and eternally.

God loves us. He desperately wants to have a relationship. But His holiness keeps us at a distance. Now, through the death and resurrected life of Jesus, we can be made holy. We must acknowledge this, believe and receive it. Then we can be made right with God. That's what I've done. I've put my faith in Jesus—and this has given me hope. I want that for you too. It won't be long. I love you.

It Won't Be Long©
Shout (Ken Tamplin & Chuck King)

Go, go, one chance to make it known,
One way to break away or the heart'll turn to stone,
Rock, rock, that's what I'm standing on,
Oh Lord, make it right, and your light'll carry on.

Won't be long, all will be made known,
Won't be long, yeah, we'll face it one by one,
Won't be long, give you hope to carry on,
Won't be long, oh, come on and sing along.

High life, they say the strong survive,
Don't care 'bout all that jive, no one makes it out alive,
Reap, sow, that stance is all I know,
One more for the curtain call, gotta face that fall alone.

Won't be long, when all will be made known,
Won't be long, yeah, we'll face it one by one,
Won't be long, give you hope to carry on,
Won't be long, are you ready?

No, it won't be long,
All the clouds roll back, and we'll be gone,
Yeah, we'll face it one by one,
Oh, come on and sing along.

Won't be long, Won't be long, Won't be long, Won't be long.[12]

Endnotes

1 **Henley, D., Campbell, M. and Souther, J. D. (1989), "The Heart of the Matter."**

Copyright © 1989 EMI Blackwood Music Inc. Woody Creek Music and Wild Gator Music

All Rights on behalf of EMI Blackwood Music Inc. Administered by Sony/ATV Music Publishing LLC, 424 Church Street, Suite 1200, Nashville, TN 37219

International Copyright Secured All Rights Reserved.
Reprinted by Permission of Hal Leonard LLC.

2 **Loy, M., Mosteller, J., Bailey, J., Rousseau, J. and Farren, M. (2017), "I Will Trust."**

Copyright © 2017 Centricity Music Publishing (ASCAP) Centricity Songs (BMI) CentricSongs (SESAC) Farren Love And War Pub (SESAC) Integrity's Alleluia! Music (SESAC) (adm. at CapitolCMGPublishing.com) All rights reserved. Used by permission.

3 **Fieldes, M., Hoagland, E. and Smith, J. (2018), "Yes I Will."**

HBC Worship Music (ASCAP) / All Essential Music (ASCAP) / Upside Down Under (BMI) / Be Essential Songs (BMI) / Hickory Bill Doc (SESAC) / So Essential Tunes (SESAC) / Jingram Music Publishing (ASCAP) / (admin at EssentialMusicPublishing.com [3]). All rights reserved. Used by permission.

4 **Loy, M., Mosteller, J., Bailey, J., Linklater, J. and Rousseau, J. (2017), "In-Between."**

Copyright © 2017 Centricity Music Publishing (ASCAP) Centricity Songs (BMI) CentricSongs (SESAC) (adm. at CapitolCMGPublishing.com) All rights reserved. Used by permission.

5 **De Coup-Crank, D., "Death Before Life."**

All rights reserved. Used by permission.

6 **Estevez, C., Guevara, L., Aranda, D., Estevez, R., Biancaniello, L. and Biancaniello, M. (2019), "Symphony."**

© 2019 Life Church Worship Publishing (BMI) (admin by Heritage Worship Music Publishing) / ISHYDVON Music (ASCAP) / Penny Farthing Music (ASCAP) /. All Rights Reserved. Used by permission.

7 **Doerksen, B. (2008), "Refiner's Fire."**

Copyright © 2008 Mercy Vineyard Publishing (ASCAP) Vineyard Songs (Canada)

(SOCAN) (adm. at CapitolCMGPublishing.com) All rights reserved. Used by permission.

8 **Loy, M., Rea, G., Mosteller, J., Bailey, J., Shust, A., Fee, S., and Rousseau, J. (2017), "Giving It All To You."**

Copyright © 2017 Centricity Music Publishing (ASCAP) Centricity Songs (BMI) CentricSongs (SESAC) Creed Love Music (BMI) (adm. at CapitolCMGPublishing.com) All rights reserved. Used by permission.

9 **Cowart, B. and Bentley, H. (2019), "I Know."**

All Essential Music (ASCAP) / Bentley Street Songs (ASCAP) / (admin at EssentialMusicPublishing.com [3]). All rights reserved. Used by permission.

10 **Lee, T. A., Sheets, L.H.W. and Wells, C.N. (2012), "Need You Now (How Many Times)."**

Lyrics © Mike Curb Music, Do Write Music LLC.

11 **Millard, B., Cochran, N., Graul, B., Glover, B., Scheuchzer, M. and Shaffer, R. (2019), "Almost Home."**

Copyright © 2019 9t One Songs (ASCAP) Ariose Music (ASCAP) (adm. at CapitolCMGPublishing.com) All rights reserved. Used by permission.

Tunes of MercyMe (SESAC) / No Sappy Music (SESAC) / (admin at EssentialMusicPublishing.com [3]). All rights reserved. Used by permission.

12 **Tamplin, K. and King, C. (1988), "It Won't Be Long."**

This song is written by Ken Tamplin and Chuck King, © 1988 Broken Songs (a div. of Meis Music Group). All rights reserved. Used by permission.